♡ Happy Birthday Annie 2013 ♡

Hope you enjoy this book. I don't know why I picked this book except that the colours are "brilliant" and the possibilities are endless.

Maybe some illustrations for your Childrens Books that you are creating? Who knows!

Enjoy ♡.

Lots of Love
Wendy ♡

ONE MILLION

# Mandalas

**For You to Create, Print, and Color**

# ONE MILLION
# Mandalas
### For You to Create, Print, and Color

## Madonna Gauding

ST. MARTIN'S GRIFFIN
NEW YORK

ONE MILLION MANDALAS

www.stmartins.com

Library of Congress Cataloging-in-Publication Data
Available Upon Request

ISBN-13: 978-0-312-57403-1
ISBN-10: 0-312-57403-7

First U.S. Edition: September 2009

10 9 8 7 6 5 4 3 2 1

Printed in China

# Contents

# Introduction

## What is a mandala?

*Mandala* is Sanskrit for "circle" or "completion." It can also mean "sacred center" or "essence container." Mandalas are closely associated with Hinduism and Buddhism, where they are used extensively in rituals and as aids for meditation. Mandalas are two-dimensional paintings of a three-dimensional sacred environment. They help practitioners learn spiritual truths, focus attention, and establish a sacred space. Mandalas symbolize the cosmos, or the universe, and encourage the appreciation of all life as sacred. They represent the dwelling place of the divine and of enlightened beings. Meditating on a mandala can help you to access progressively deeper levels of the unconscious, ultimately assisting you to experience a mystical sense of oneness with the cosmos or a higher being.

Because mandalas represent the presence of the sacred in everyday life, they can remind you of the sanctity of the universe and your potential for ongoing personal and spiritual development. This unique book and CD-ROM will allow you to print and color one million mandalas created from combinations of one hundred outer rings, middle rings, and inner discs. Working with these mandalas will help you to achieve your own personal peace through the simple, concentrated, and meditative act of coloring.

*below* **A Buddhist mandala. The outer ring symbolizes the purifying fire of wisdom; the inner ring represents the stages of realizing enlightenment; and the center, the realization of enlightenment.**

## Mandalas East and West

Of all the Eastern traditions, Tibetan Buddhism has made the most extensive use of the mandala for spiritual development. A *kyil khor* (Tibetan for mandala) in Vajrayana Buddhism usually depicts the sacred landscape and dwelling place of the Buddha or an enlightened being. Such mandalas consist of an outer ring, an inner circle (or square), and an ornately decorated mandala palace at the center. The outer circle represents separation and protection from the outer everyday or samsaric world—the world of suffering and eternal reincarnation. It often depicts a protective ring of fire symbolizing the purifying fire of wisdom. The middle circle or circles depict various stages in the process of realization of enlightenment. The center represents the realization of enlightenment, often depicted as a Buddha or enlightened being. Practitioners mentally visualize entering the mandala and becoming one with the Buddha residing in the center. In this way they visualize their own enlightenment. All the mandalas in this book follow this basic "outer, middle, and center" layout principle.

In the Christian tradition, the mandala appears in the famous rose windows in cathedrals such as Notre Dame and Chartes in France, or St. John the Divine in New York City. In the Middle Ages, the Church created spectacular jewel-like rose windows to instruct the faithful in the liturgy and encourage meditation on its meaning. Most often Christ or Mary occupied the center, with the outer circles depicting various truths and symbols of the Christian faith. They could include the Trinity—the Father, Son, and Holy Spirit—the life of Christ, or portraits of the twelve Apostles, all constructed using brilliant pieces of stained glass. Other themes included the story of creation, astrological signs and symbols, and symbols of the Catholic Church, such as the *agnus dei*, or Lamb of God, the orb surmounted by a cross, or the alpha and omega. Virtues and vices were illustrated for reminders of what to embrace and what to avoid. Just to gaze on these beautiful windows was an awe-inspiring experience, taking visitors to the cathedral out of their everyday lives and providing them with deep joy and spiritual inspiration. As in the Eastern tradition, the rose windows reminded the faithful of the sacredness of all life and the importance of embracing one's potential for spiritual development.

# Symbolism

## Mandalas as symbols of nature

The mandala represents the circle, the primal form of the universe itself. The sun and moon are circles as are the billions of stars in the night sky. The earth itself is a huge ball hurtling through space, circling around the fiery orb of our life-giving sun. The rounded forms of atoms and cells endlessly combine to create the myriad forms of existence. A flower, a snowflake, a cross-section of a tree—each reveals growth moving outward from a central point. The Hindus called this point a *bindu*, or sacred point—the source from which everything that exists emanates. Modern physics speculates that the universe came into existence from the "Big Bang," an explosion from a single primeval atom, which may have simultaneously embodied both form and formlessness. Mathematicians also tell us that a circle has a center, but the point at the center of the circle is dimensionless. The mandala symbolizes the ineffable sacredness at the center of everyday reality. That sacredness, the center of the circle, is boundless and eternal with no beginning and no end.

Because mandalas symbolize the source of all reality, coloring a mandala can evoke the contemplation of existential questions about the origin and meaning of life. You may find yourself thinking about the origin of the universe, and if it still has its original center. You may wonder if it will continue to expand indefinitely or if it exists on several planes at once. The great photographs from the Hubble Space Telescope may come to mind, showing in awesome detail the spiral galaxies and circular movement of the planets.

On a more mundane level, coloring mandalas may lead you to take more interest in preparing your evening meal as you examine the mandala like circles in the melon, the apple, or the concentric rings in a slice of onion. You may enjoy examining the mandala shapes in your garden, in the plant forms and shapes of insects, and in the tree rings on your cut firewood. The mandala is everywhere in nature and as you color mandalas you will begin to notice them all around you.

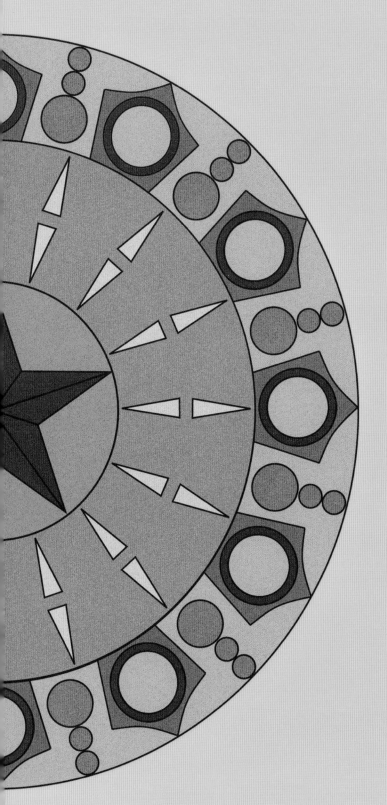

## Mandalas as symbols of community

We human beings have always organized ourselves into mandala-like communities. Perhaps it started when our ancient ancestors gathered in a circle around the fire, and then, in a spontaneous moment, began to dance around it. Most cultures around the world have a circle dance of some kind, where the mandala is danced in celebration of a wedding or a feast day. We have our family circles and our circles of friends. Our close circles are protective and nurturing and familiar. We circle around when there is difficulty or when we want to celebrate. We form our nightly circles around the family dinner table.

We also participate in social circles built around our institutions that function as magnets drawing people from around our community. We go to the local pub; we attend church; we take our kids to school. We create prayer circles, healing circles, investment circles, knitting circles, and reading circles. We sit in a circle to discuss the books we've read. We form human mandalas as naturally and effortlessly as an apple seed produces an apple. We need our human mandalas to live a rich and fulfilling life.

# Symbolism

## Mandalas as symbols of time

In the Hindu tradition, Shiva, the Hindu god, is depicted dancing in the center of a flaming mandala. He occupies the center of the universe. He is Creator, Preserver, and Destroyer. In his dance of ecstasy he imparts the lesson that life is cyclical and impermanent. Nothing in this life lasts, but in accepting that reality we are freed to live life more fully.

Life is dominated by cycles. We are born, we grow up, we mature, and we die. Everything in nature follows this trajectory, as do most man-made institutions and cultures. Whole civilizations have come and gone, as have entire species. We no longer have wooly mammoths tromping through the garden, and we may soon, thanks to our short-sightedness, no longer have the polar bear or tiger. The stock market balloons and then crashes, taking with it our hard-earned savings. The seasons come and go without our really noticing and the years seem to pass more quickly. The mandala reminds us of the cyclical nature of time, and that nothing in life is static or permanent. Whether we like it or not, change is constant and life is unpredictable.

Living in urban environments or even in rural areas, we spend too much time indoors, watching TV or sitting in front of our computers. We miss the swelling and thinning of the moon, the rising and setting of the sun, the passing of cloud formations, even the passing of the seasons. We notice it is colder outside so we put on a jacket, but we may have missed the subtle color change of the leaves and the scrambling of the squirrels for nuts to store for winter. Lost in a cloud of electronic stimulation, we lose sight of the subtle cycles of nature, and the cycles of our own lives. And of course, there never seems to be enough time in the day to get everything done.

*left*
**Natural mandalas are all around us. You may find you begin to notice them more as you color your mandalas.**

*right*
**Coloring mandalas will help you to slow down and reconnect to the cyclical nature of time, the rhythms of nature, and the reality of change.**

# Emotional Healing

*below*
**These modern mandalas
have been digitally colored.**

## Mandalas as tools for emotional healing

A mandala is basically any plan, chart, or geometric pattern that represents the cosmos or the universe. It can also represent the Self as a microcosm of the universe. The mandala was fascinating to the Swiss psychoanalyst Carl Jung (1875–1961) who saw it as "a representation of the unconscious self." He explored mandalas from Hindu and Buddhist traditions and eventually began to create and color mandalas of his own design. He found this practice allowed him to access the images and energy of his unconscious mind, which helped him in his spiritual and psychological growth. He defined the unconscious mind as a storehouse of universal archetypes—the themes and images common to every time and culture. Typical archetypes manifest in universal themes such as birth, death, marriage, or betrayal—the stuff of dreams, myths, fairy tales, and religious symbolism. There are also archetypal roles that are recognized around the world such as mother, father, old man, old woman, child, and orphan.

After his own extensive exploration of the mandala, he had his patients draw and paint mandalas. By "reading" their mandalas, he was able to diagnose their emotional and psychological problems. At the same time, the act of drawing and coloring mandalas over time was highly therapeutic and helped his patients develop the wholeness and integration they needed to heal. His patients' use of images and symbols, whether abstract or figural, helped them come to terms with the various warring aspects of their psyche, encouraging acceptance and healing. The mandala contained repressed memories and desires, current issues, as well as hopes and fears for the future. It represented the whole person, that is: past, present, and future contained in a sacred healing environment.

## How coloring mandalas can help you

The act of coloring the circular mandala, whether you draw it yourself or not, helps you bypass your conscious mind (your left brain), and access your intuition (your right brain). If you need to solve a problem or find out what you really think of a person or situation, coloring a mandala can help you sort it out. If you want to explore your psyche on a deeper lever, coloring a mandala can help you access your hopes and fears, and your hidden thoughts and feelings. As the ancients understood, the mandala is an excellent tool for focusing, centering, and accessing our deepest and highest natures. It also helps us comprehend the universe and our daily lives as precious and sacred.

Many people find coloring mandalas while listening to music or even watching TV relaxing and pleasurable. Working with mandalas in this way can be a beneficial stress reliever. If you want to enhance your work with mandalas, the following pages introduce you to meditations to use while coloring mandalas that will promote psychological and spiritual growth. Focusing and meditating while you color a mandala can unleash their transformative power.

If you choose to meditate while coloring any of these million mandalas, set aside time to be alone in a quiet space. Make sure you are comfortable and set aside enough time to complete the mandala. When you finish you may want to write down any insights or realizations you may have had in a journal. The journal should be large enough to allow you to paste your mandala next to your notes if you choose to do that. After trying a few of these meditations, you may want to try creating your own.

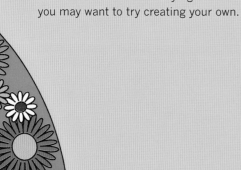
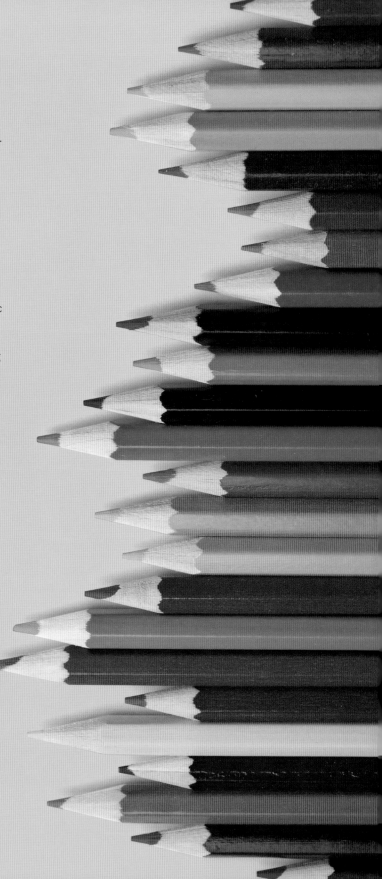

# Mandala Meditations

## Calming and centering

- Close your eyes, take a few deep breaths, and try to clear your mind of any thoughts. Simply concentrate on your breathing for a few minutes.

- Open your eyes and select a pre-drawn mandala or create your own mandala by choosing an outer, middle, and inner ring. Choose a mandala or create a mandala that feels soothing and restful for you.

- Now print out your mandala and color it with colored pencils, or any other traditional media.

- Beginning at the outer ring, work your way to the center. Choose colors that you find calming and harmonious.

- As you color your mandala, try to focus on your breath and when your mind wanders—and it will—gently bring your focus back to your breathing.

- When you complete your mandala, notice if you feel more calm and centered than when you began this process. Print out your mandala and place it where you can admire it. Let it remind you that you can calm and center yourself at any time you choose.

## Your outer, inner, and secret self

- In this meditation you will create your own mandala by selecting an outer ring, a middle ring, and a center (inner ring).

- Begin by choosing an outer ring that represents the face you show the world, and which represents your social self, or your public persona.

- Next, choose a middle ring that represents what you consider your deeper nature or "who you really are." You may let your friends and loved ones see this deeper more vulnerable side of yourself.

- Finally, choose a center. The center is your secret, most private self. This self you rarely, if ever, share with anyone. This self may be somewhat of a mystery to you as well. The most secret self can be a source of hidden treasure. It can hold talents and gifts waiting to be developed, or love and compassion waiting to be expressed toward yourself and others. It may also hold old wounds from your past waiting to be addressed and healed.

- Meditate on the three aspects of yourself as you color your mandala from the outside toward the center. As you color, generate a feeling of acceptance for your outer, inner, and secret selves.

*right*
**A monk meditates outdoors. Meditating while coloring mandalas can unleash their transformative power, helping to promote spiritual and psychological growth.**

# Mandala Meditations

## Weathering a storm

- Choose this meditation if you are experiencing a personal crisis, such as losing your job, your spouse, or partner; grieving for a loved one who has passed on; or if you are simply having a bad day.

- Choose a pre-drawn mandala or create your own.

- Set the intention that coloring this mandala will help you move through this rough patch. Allow your feelings of fear, anger, sadness, or grief, and also of hope to emerge. Choose colors that express these emotions.

- As you color, meditate on the fact that this difficult challenge you are experiencing today is itself impermanent. Consider that a crisis, however painful, can also bring opportunity and that time can be a healer. If you are simply having a bad day, allow coloring your mandala to cheer your outlook.

## One person wearing many hats

- Consider all the roles you play in life—such as daughter or son, parent, worker, friend, community member, lover, or spouse—and your responsibilities in those roles.

- Create a mandala that represents how you feel about managing all these roles in your life. If your roles seem integrated, choose designs that feel harmonious. If you feel your various roles are warring, choose designs that suggest that feeling.

- Choose colors that repeat in the outer ring, middle ring, and center of your mandala. Try to integrate all three parts of the mandala using repeated color schemes.

- When you complete your mandala, visualize all your life roles functioning in an integrated, whole, and harmonious way.

*below*
**Choose colors and color schemes that express the emotions you are feeling.**

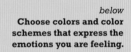

## Manifesting your best self

- Create your own mandala by choosing an outer ring that represents how you function at this stage of your life, a middle ring that represents your intention to confront your issues and negative habitual patterns, and an inner ring that represents your highest self, the person you can be or would like to be.

- Start coloring from the outside ring and work your way to the center.

- As you color, think about the person you would like to become. What values do you want to embody, what negative patterns in your life would you like to transform? How do you want to be of service to yourself and your family and friends? How can you serve the universe with your life?

- When you finish, meditate on the person you would like to be and commit to actions that will help you become that person.

## Manifesting what you desire

- Choose a mandala or create a mandala that feels right to you for what you would like to manifest. Intend that this manifestation will be positive for you and not harmful in any way for others.

- Begin coloring from the outside and work in to the center.

- As you color, visualize what you would like to manifest—a job, a relationship, a house, or something as simple as a book, or a new pair of shoes. Feel what it would be like to have it and imagine it in as much detail as you can.

- When you finish coloring, hang it in a prominent place in your home where you can see it on a daily basis until you manifest what you desire.

# Using the Book and CD

This book lets you design your own mandalas by choosing combinations of ring patterns, which can then be colored and used for meditation. There are 100 inner rings, 100 middle rings, and 100 outer rings, allowing for a million different mandalas.

The gallery section of this book shows just some of the mandalas that can be made, and you can use it to help you pick designs or specific ring patterns for you to use in your own mandalas. You can use this gallery section as your sketchbook, and color directly onto the page, or you could recreate the design using the CD and print out the artwork.

Each mandala in the gallery lists which Inner, Middle, and Outer ring complete the design, so you can easily find a particular ring pattern on the CD.

**Outer: 27**
**Middle: 6**
**Inner: 22**

# Creating mandalas

Insert the disc into your computer. First, read the license agreement. You must agree to the terms before using the program. Then click on the launch program option and the Mandalas window should appear on your screen.

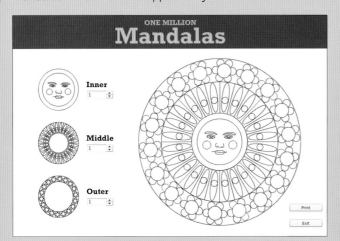

Simply scroll through the options for your Inner, Middle, and Outer ring using the up and down arrows until you are happy with the complete mandala design. If you see a ring you like, but want to scroll through the rest of the options, make a note of the ring number so you can go back to it.

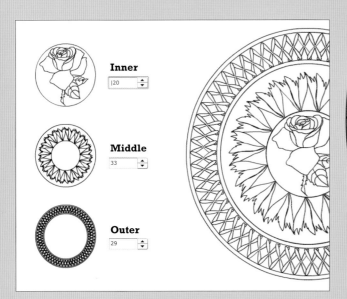

Alternatively, you could search for a specific ring by number. If there is a ring you have seen in the gallery that you would like to use for your mandala, simply put your cursor over the box, enter its corresponding number, and press return on your keyboard.

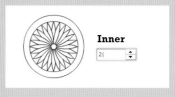

Once you are happy with your finished design, select Print.

Print

# Display

There are endless ways to enjoy your colored mandala, so let your imagination be your guide. You may want to display it in some way so you can appreciate it yourself or share it with others. Hang it informally on your refrigerator or on a bulletin board, or frame it nicely for more permanent display. If the mandala is more personal and you want to continue to view it while you digest the messages it gives you, mount it in a special sketchbook or scrapbook where it will be safe and you can view it in privacy.

If you keep your mandala in digital form by scanning it onto your computer, you can use it as a screensaver or email it to friends. Consider creating a blog with one of the free blog websites such as blogger.com, blogspot.com, or wordpress.com, and share your mandalas with the world along with what you have learned from them.

Search the Web for inexpensive or free software for creating your own calendar. Choose twelve of your favorite mandalas and create an inspiring calendar for yourself or for giving as gifts. Consider printing your mandalas on card stock and create greeting cards to send friends and family.

# The Mandalas

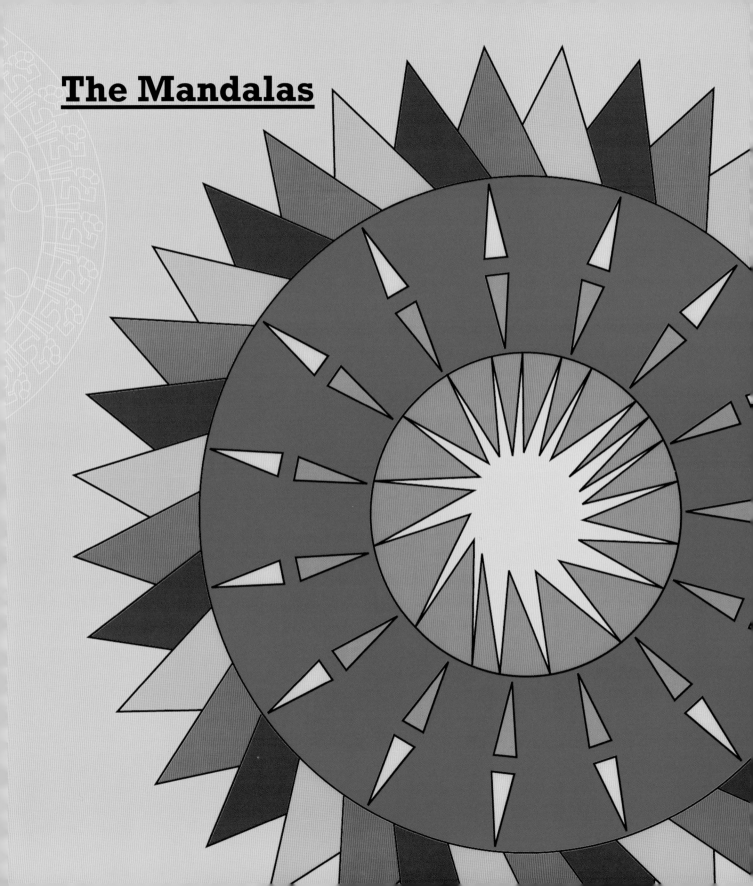

# The Mandalas

**Outer: 29**
**Middle: 7**
**Inner: 3**

**Outer: 35**
**Middle: 14**
**Inner: 29**

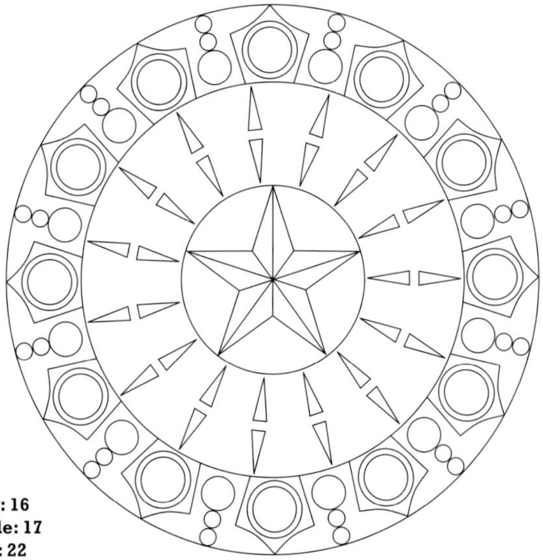

**Outer: 16**
**Middle: 17**
**Inner: 22**

Outer: 34
Middle: 11
Inner: 23

Outer: 19
Middle: 8
Inner: 29

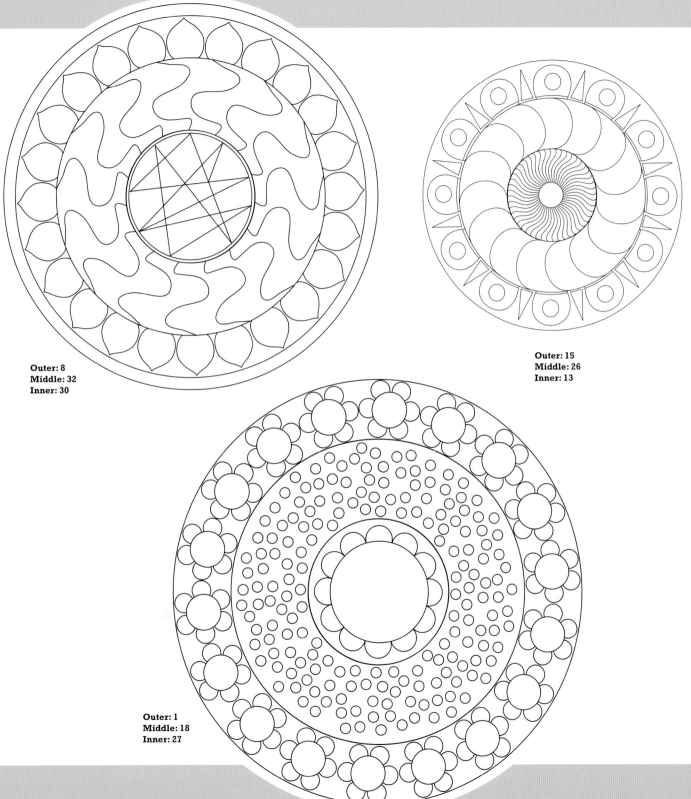

**Outer:** 8
**Middle:** 32
**Inner:** 30

**Outer:** 15
**Middle:** 26
**Inner:** 13

**Outer:** 1
**Middle:** 18
**Inner:** 27

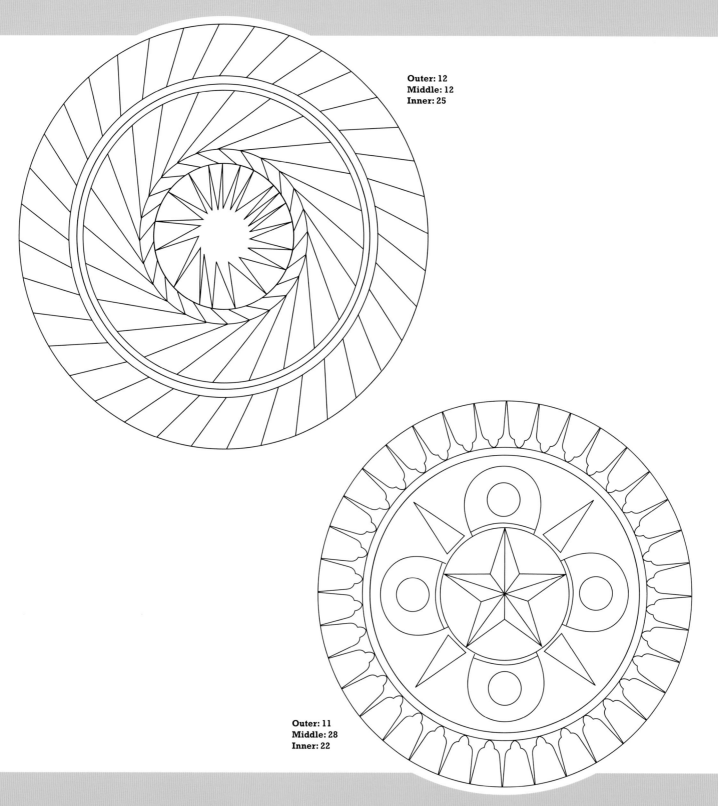

**Outer: 12**
**Middle: 12**
**Inner: 25**

**Outer: 11**
**Middle: 28**
**Inner: 22**

Outer: 1
Middle: 26
Inner: 34

Outer: 23
Middle: 05
Inner: 19

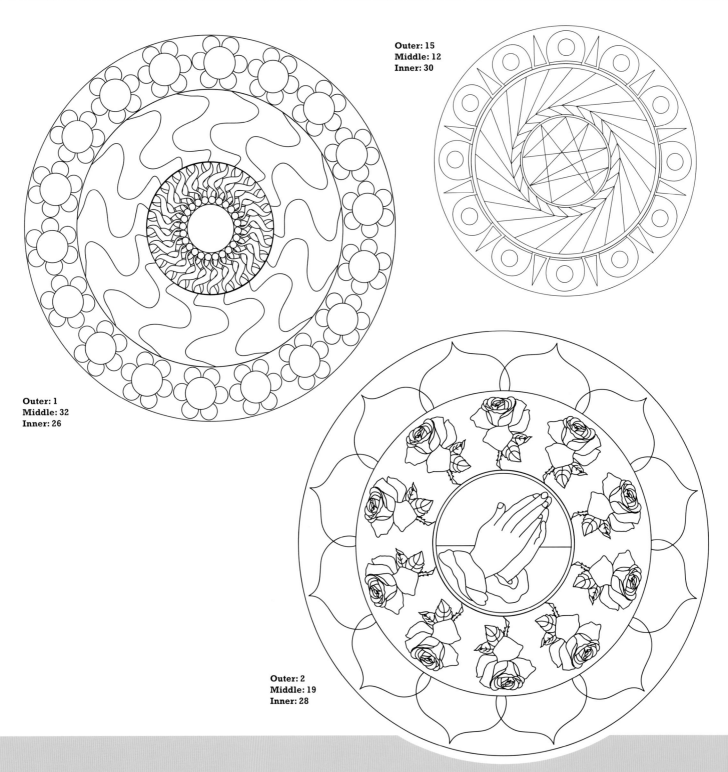

**Outer:** 15
**Middle:** 12
**Inner:** 30

**Outer:** 1
**Middle:** 32
**Inner:** 26

**Outer:** 2
**Middle:** 19
**Inner:** 28

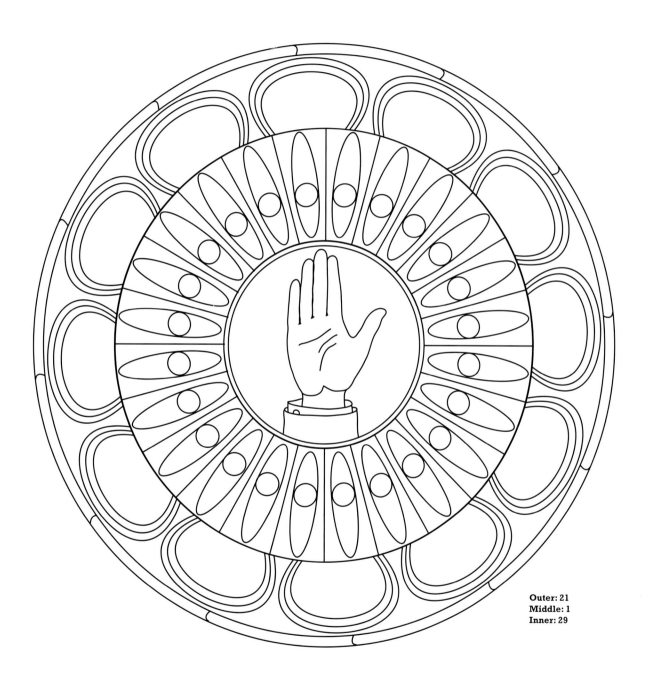

Outer: 21
Middle: 1
Inner: 29

Outer: 20
Middle: 9
Inner: 4

Outer: 25
Middle: 6
Inner: 31

Outer: 34
Middle: 7
Inner: 16

Outer: 23
Middle: 15
Inner: 29

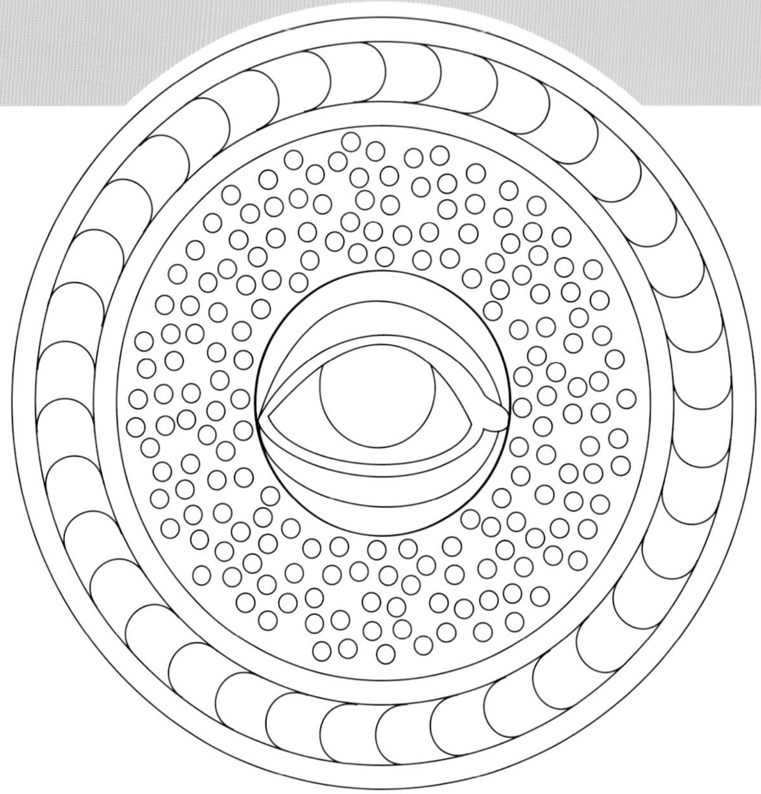

Outer: 28
Middle: 18
Inner: 23

Outer: 5
Middle: 12
Inner: 3

Outer: 8
Middle: 22
Inner: 28

Outer: 34
Middle: 20
Inner: 21

Outer: 25
Middle: 8
Inner: 4

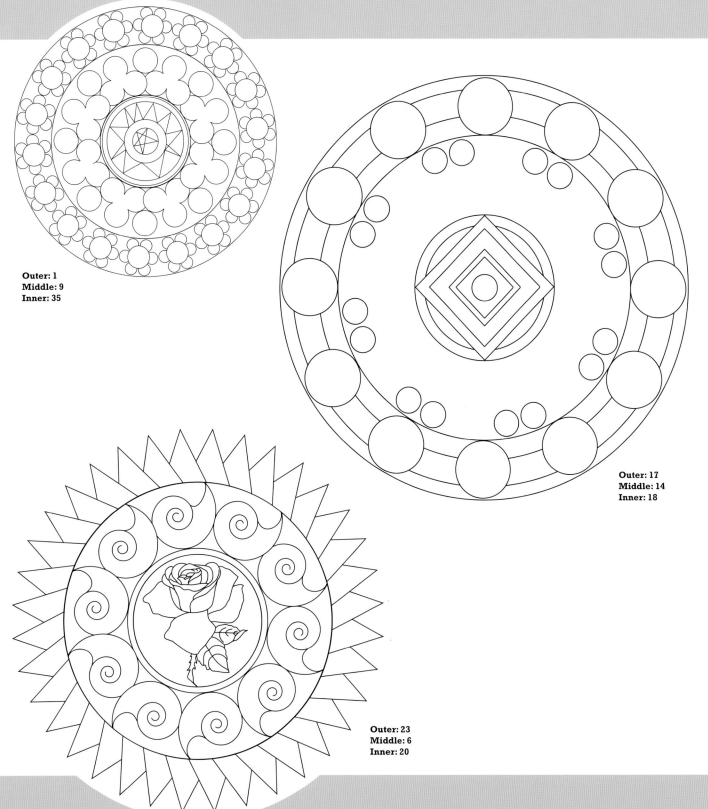

Outer: 1
Middle: 9
Inner: 35

Outer: 17
Middle: 14
Inner: 18

Outer: 23
Middle: 6
Inner: 20

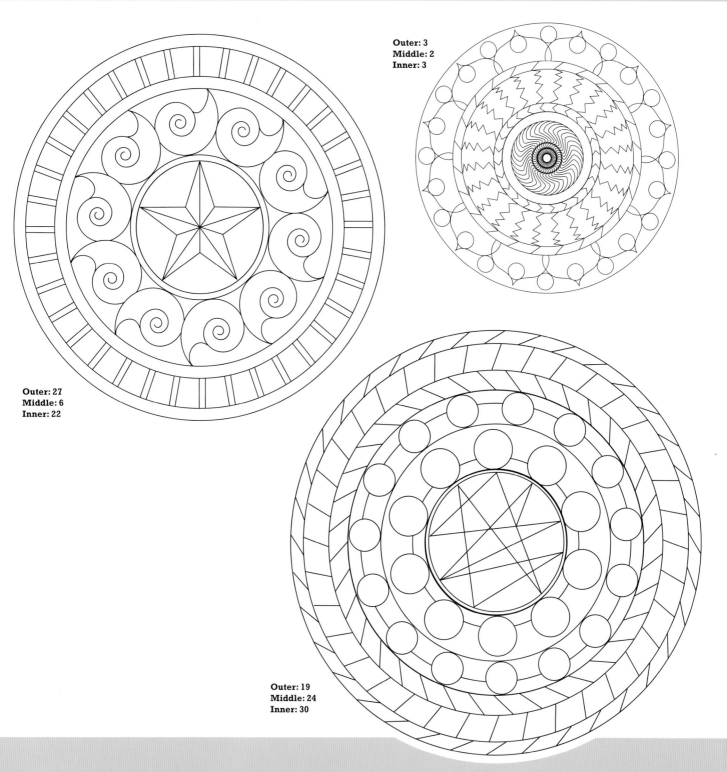

Outer: 3
Middle: 2
Inner: 3

Outer: 27
Middle: 6
Inner: 22

Outer: 19
Middle: 24
Inner: 30

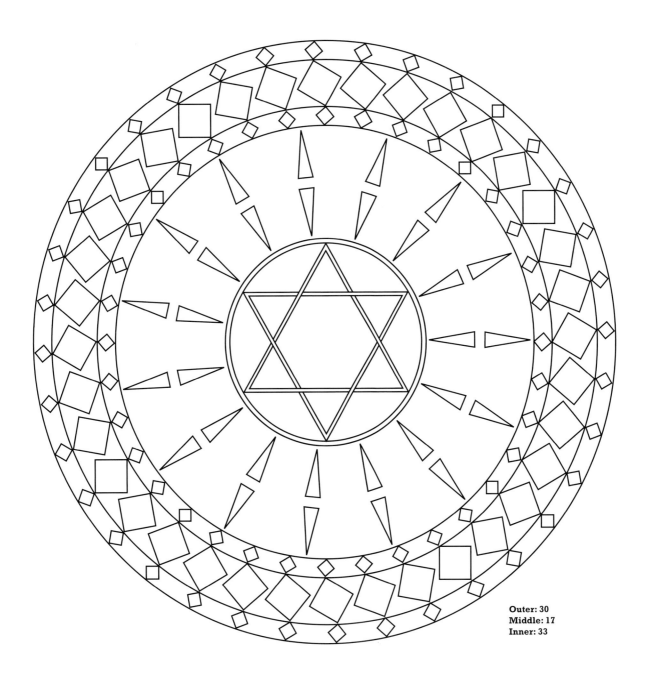

Outer: 30
Middle: 17
Inner: 33

Outer: 23
Middle: 4
Inner: 34

Outer: 21
Middle: 5
Inner: 31

Outer: 11
Middle: 14
Inner: 26

Outer: 29
Middle: 19
Inner: 17

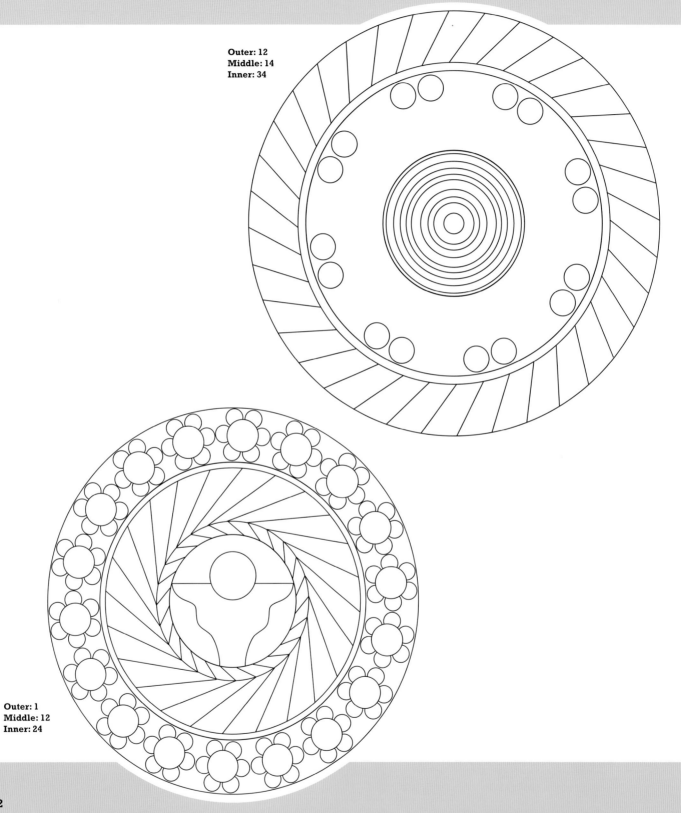

**Outer: 12**
**Middle: 14**
**Inner: 34**

**Outer: 1**
**Middle: 12**
**Inner: 24**

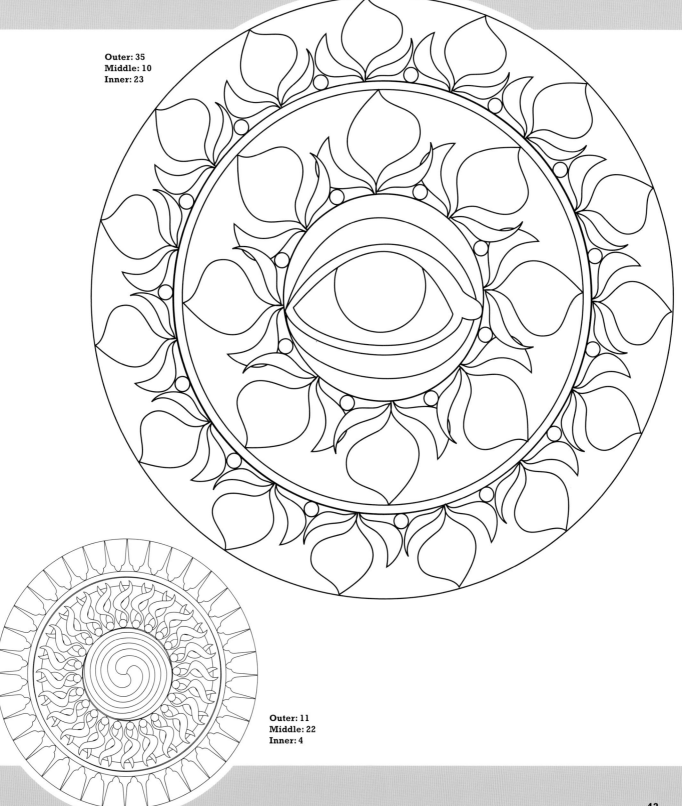

Outer: 35
Middle: 10
Inner: 23

Outer: 11
Middle: 22
Inner: 4

Outer: 30
Middle: 21
Inner: 22

Outer: 32
Middle: 5
Inner: 14

Outer: 20
Middle: 10
Inner: 13

Outer: 28
Middle: 28
Inner: 4

**Outer: 5**
**Middle: 6**
**Inner: 4**

**Outer: 34**
**Middle: 2**
**Inner: 16**

**Outer: 8**
**Middle: 7**
**Inner: 20**

Outer: 17
Middle: 20
Inner: 19

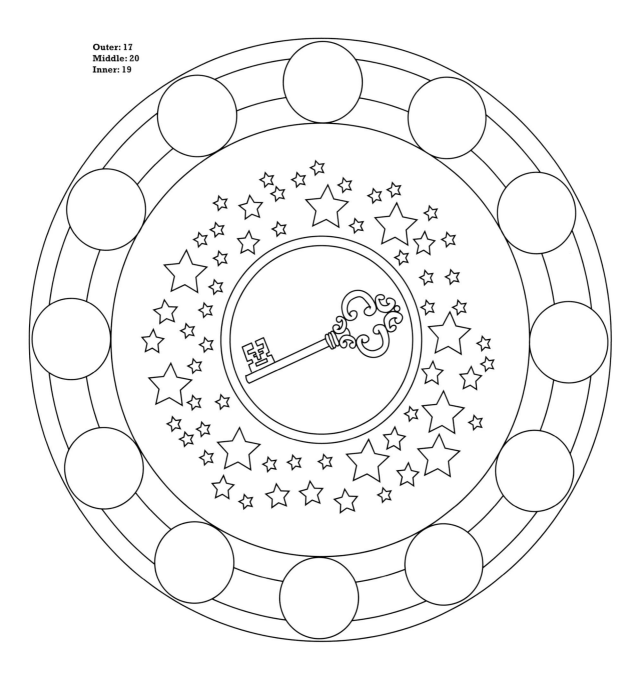

**Outer:** 4
**Middle:** 14
**Inner:** 22

Outer: 27
Middle: 12
Inner: 35

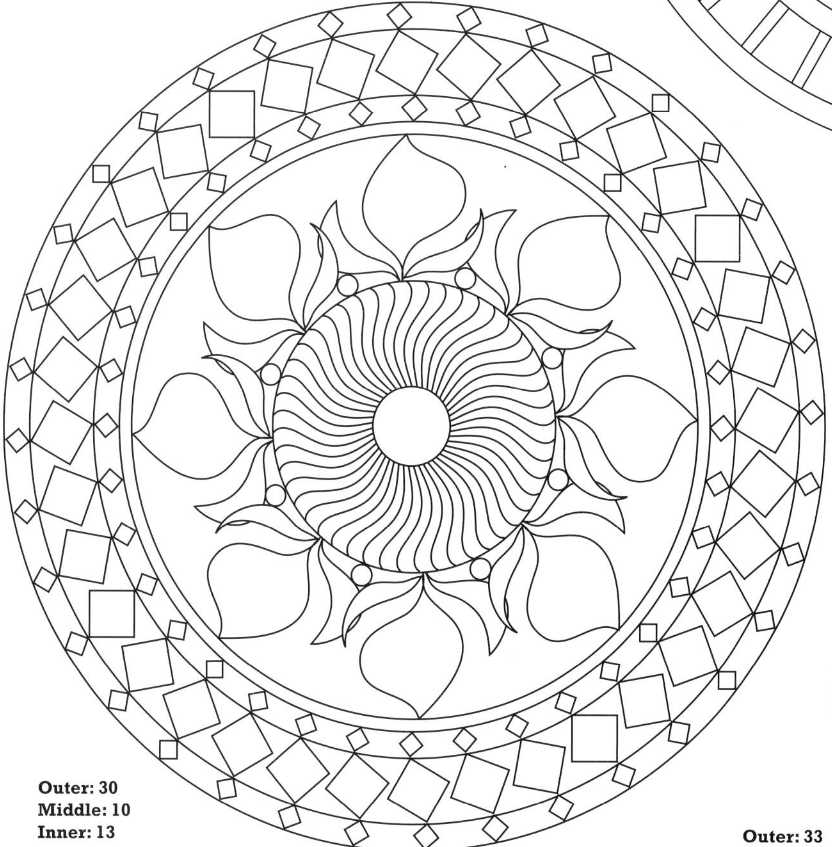

Outer: 30
Middle: 10
Inner: 13

Outer: 33
Middle: 6
Inner: 25

**Outer: 32**
**Middle: 29**
**Inner: 16**

**Outer: 11**
**Middle: 22**
**Inner: 4**

**Outer: 35**
**Middle: 16**
**Inner: 19**

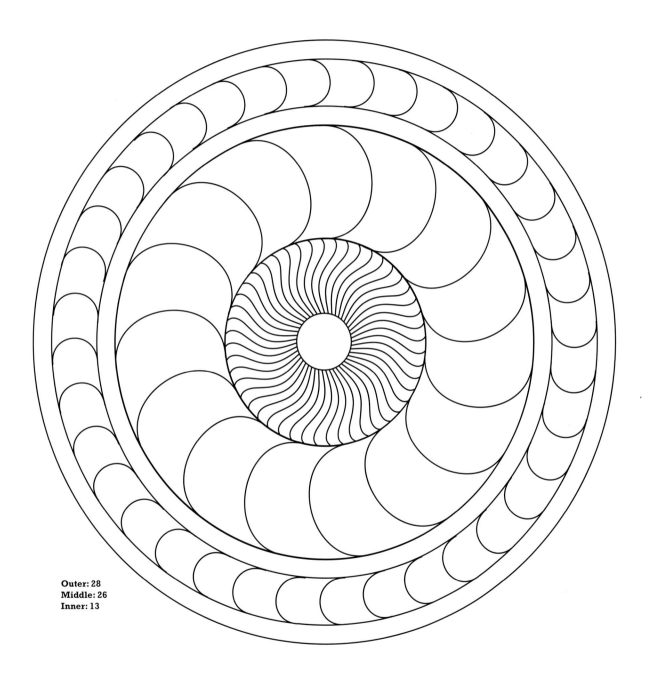

Outer: 28
Middle: 26
Inner: 13

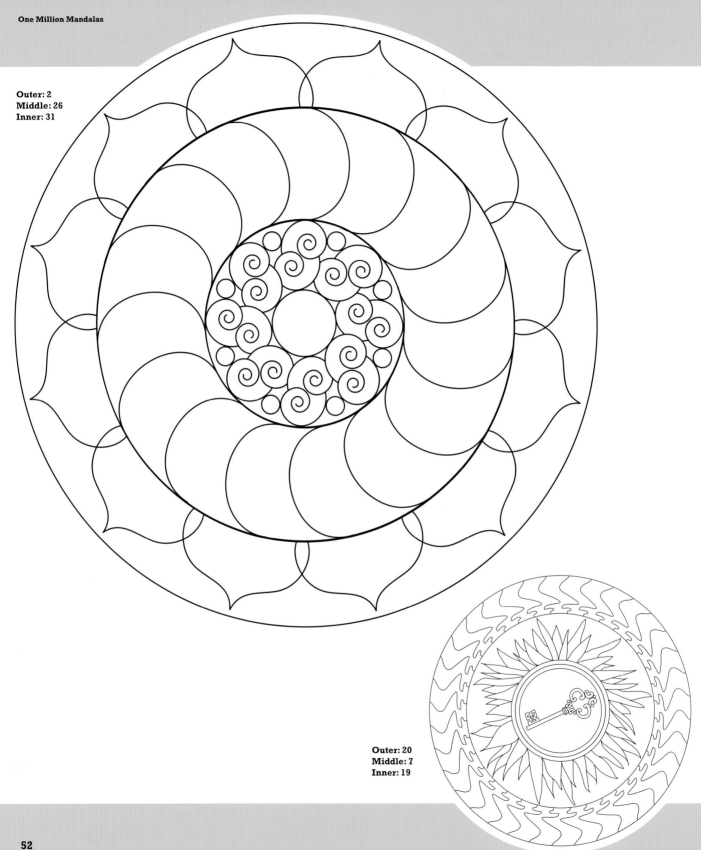

**Outer:** 2
**Middle:** 26
**Inner:** 31

**Outer:** 20
**Middle:** 7
**Inner:** 19

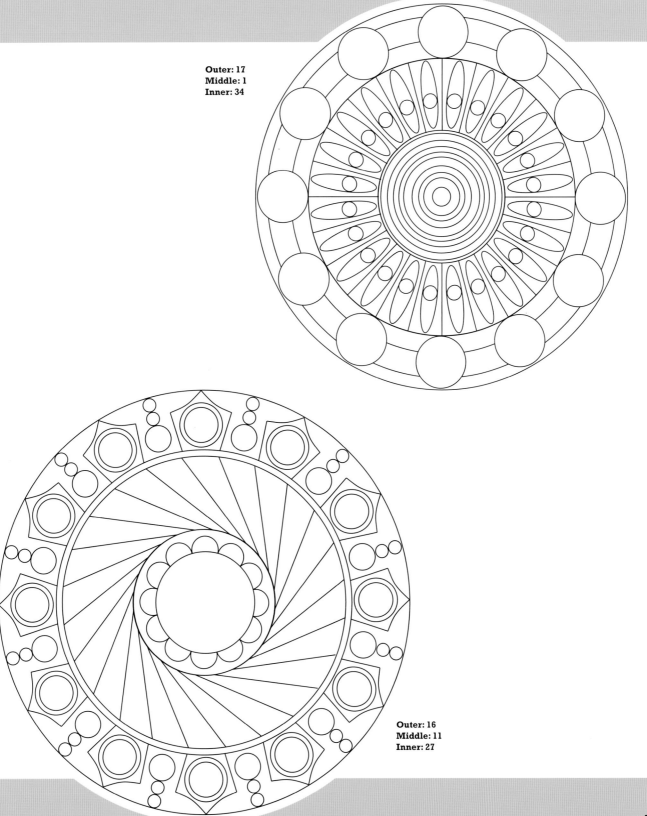

Outer: 17
Middle: 1
Inner: 34

Outer: 16
Middle: 11
Inner: 27

**Outer:** 28
**Middle:** 3
**Inner:** 34

**Outer:** 18
**Middle:** 5
**Inner:** 20

**Outer:** 11
**Middle:** 21
**Inner:** 4

Outer: 16
Middle: 29
Inner: 35

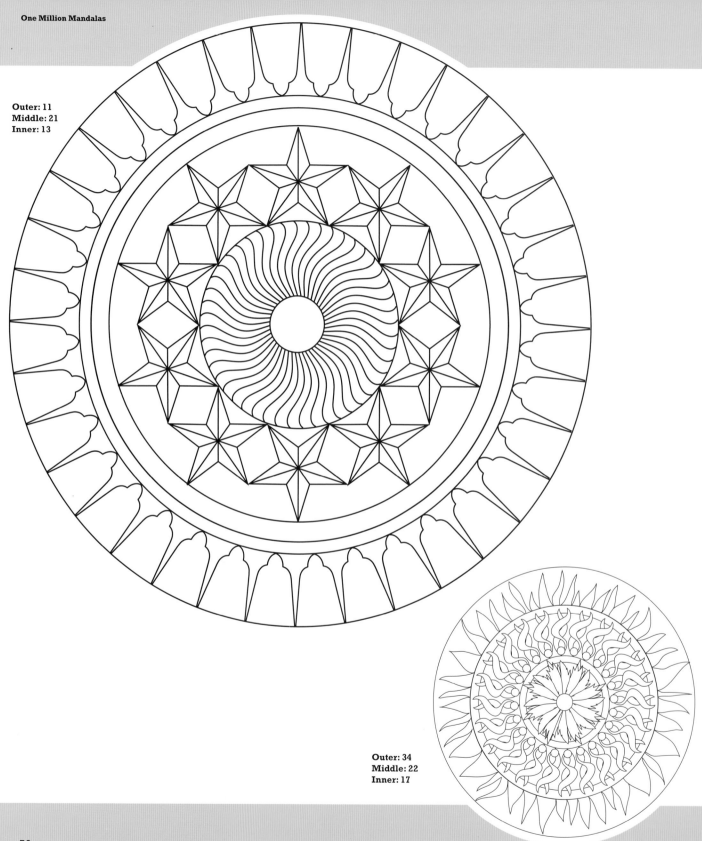

Outer: 11
Middle: 21
Inner: 13

Outer: 34
Middle: 22
Inner: 17

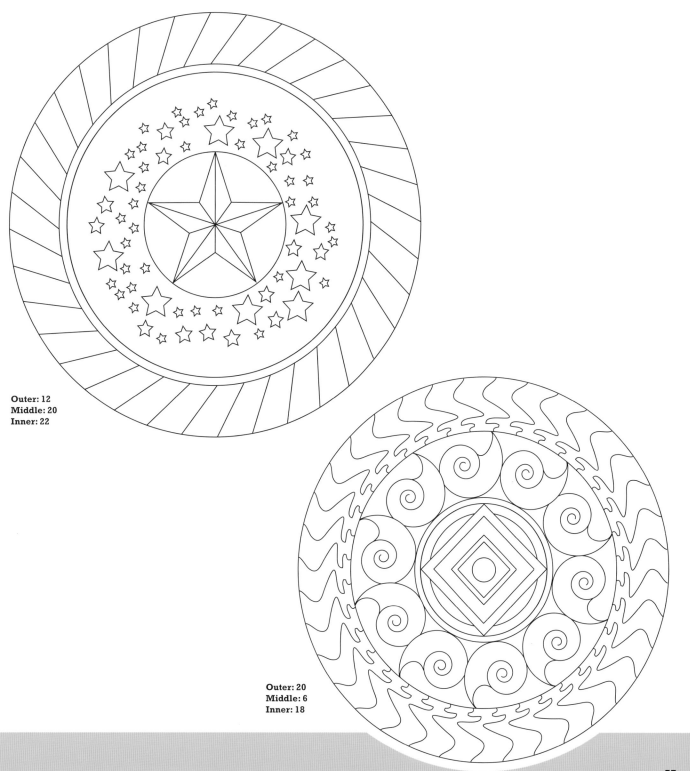

Outer: 12
Middle: 20
Inner: 22

Outer: 20
Middle: 6
Inner: 18

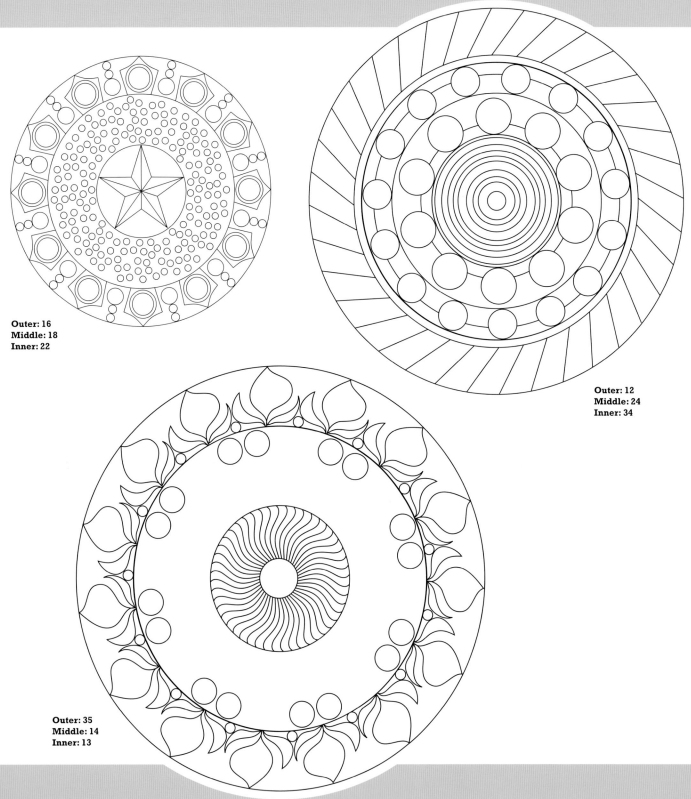

Outer: 16
Middle: 18
Inner: 22

Outer: 12
Middle: 24
Inner: 34

Outer: 35
Middle: 14
Inner: 13

Outer: 15
Middle: 17
Inner: 3

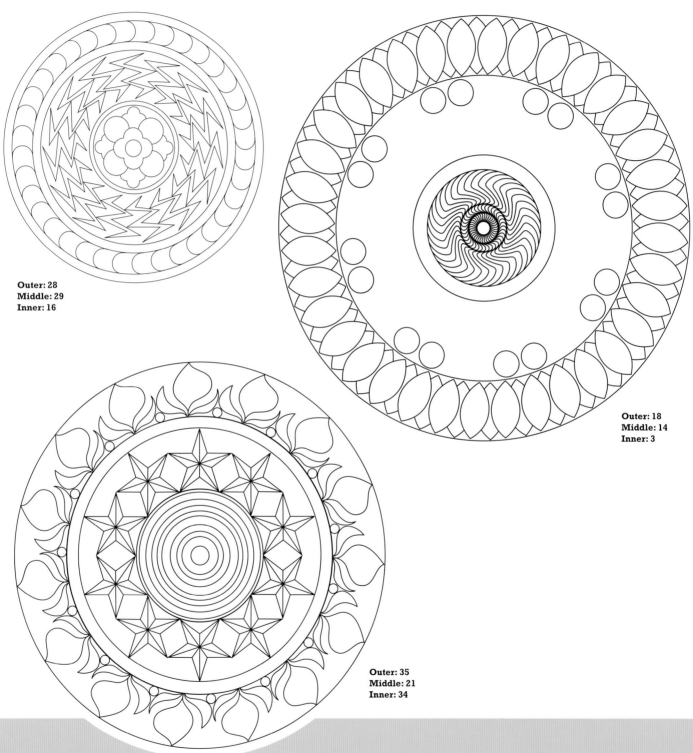

Outer: 28
Middle: 29
Inner: 16

Outer: 18
Middle: 14
Inner: 3

Outer: 35
Middle: 21
Inner: 34

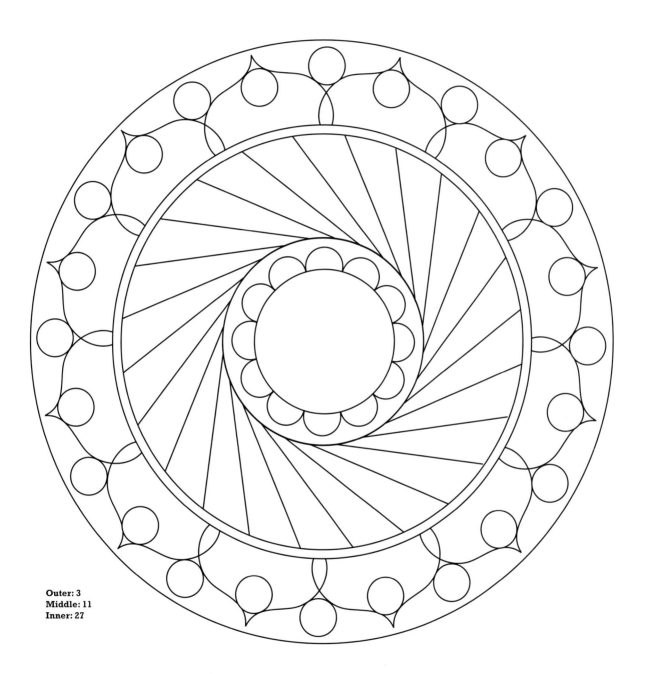

Outer: 3
Middle: 11
Inner: 27

Outer: 16
Middle: 17
Inner: 22

Outer: 14
Middle: 7
Inner: 34

Outer: 31
Middle: 12
Inner: 28

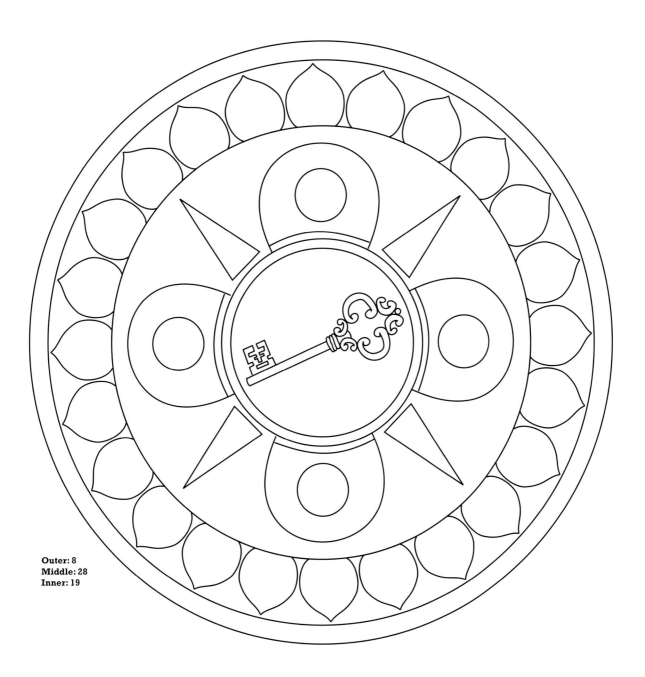

Outer: 8
Middle: 28
Inner: 19

Outer: 29
Middle: 5
Inner: 26

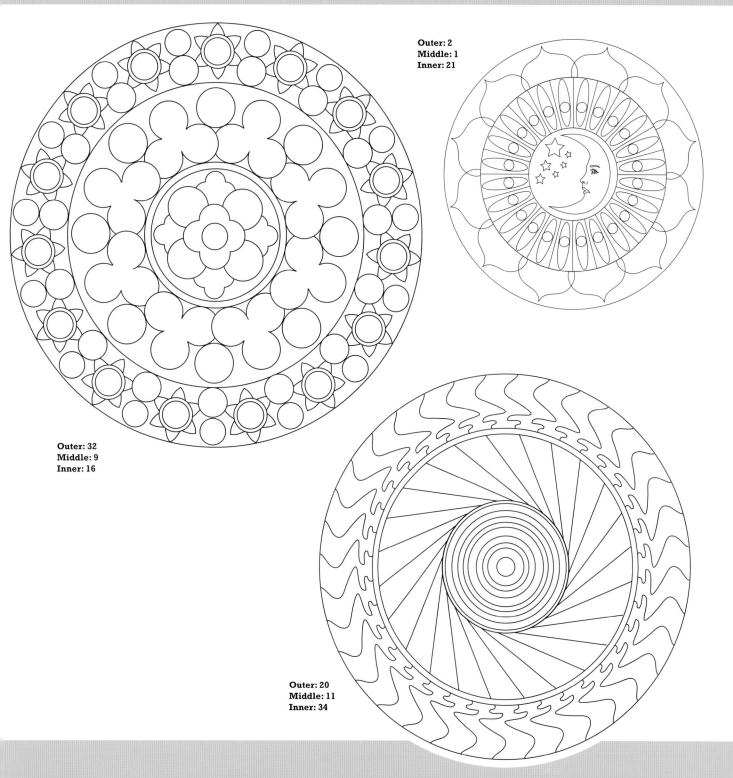

Outer: 2
Middle: 1
Inner: 21

Outer: 32
Middle: 9
Inner: 16

Outer: 20
Middle: 11
Inner: 34

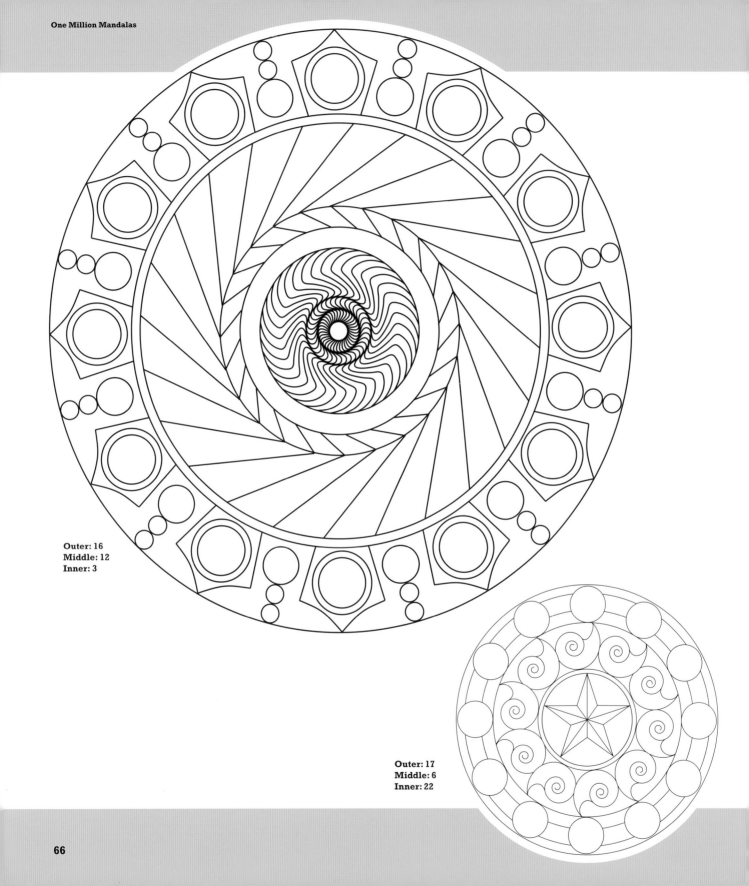

Outer: 16
Middle: 12
Inner: 3

Outer: 17
Middle: 6
Inner: 22

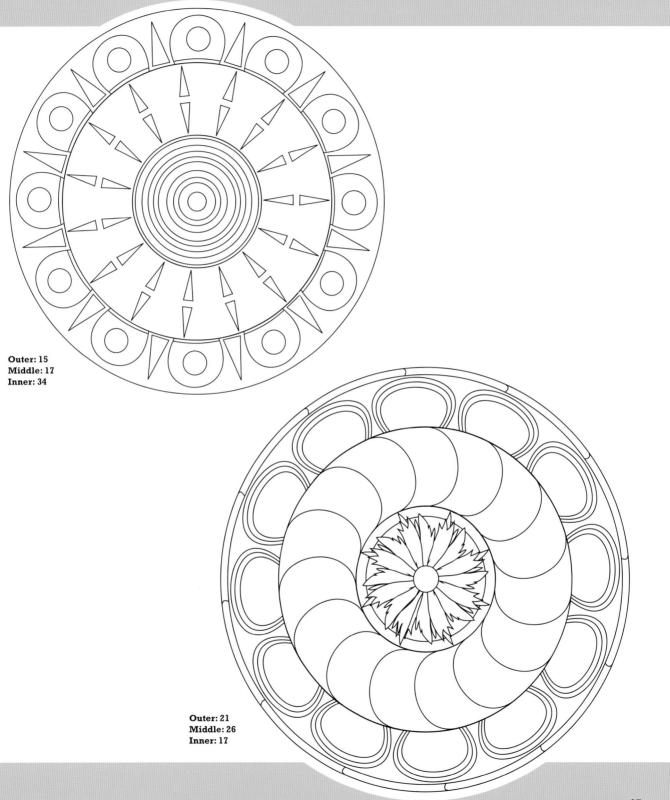

Outer: 15
Middle: 17
Inner: 34

Outer: 21
Middle: 26
Inner: 17

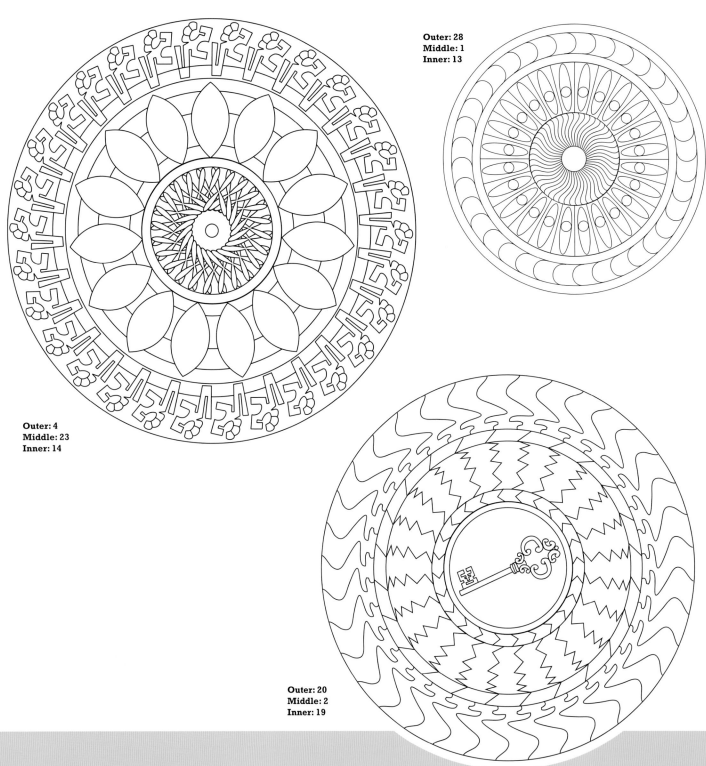

Outer: 28
Middle: 1
Inner: 13

Outer: 4
Middle: 23
Inner: 14

Outer: 20
Middle: 2
Inner: 19

Outer: 5
Middle: 8
Inner: 20

**Outer:** 15
**Middle:** 28
**Inner:** 11

Outer: 21
Middle: 5
Inner: 18

Outer: 19
Middle: 16
Inner: 17

Outer: 32
Middle: 23
Inner: 34

**Outer:** 5
**Middle:** 11
**Inner:** 29

**Outer:** 20
**Middle:** 8
**Inner:** 27

**Outer:** 18
**Middle:** 23
**Inner:** 20

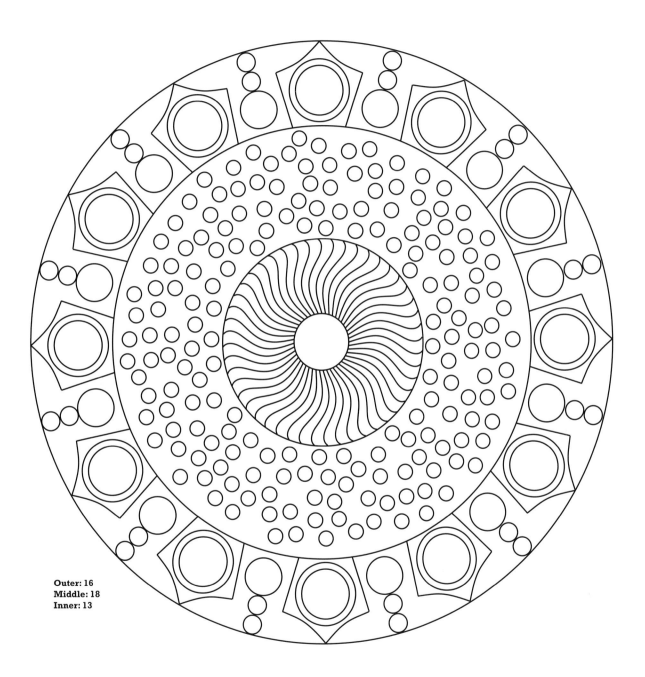

Outer: 16
Middle: 18
Inner: 13

Outer: 15
Middle: 22
Inner: 18

Outer: 21
Middle: 12
Inner: 35

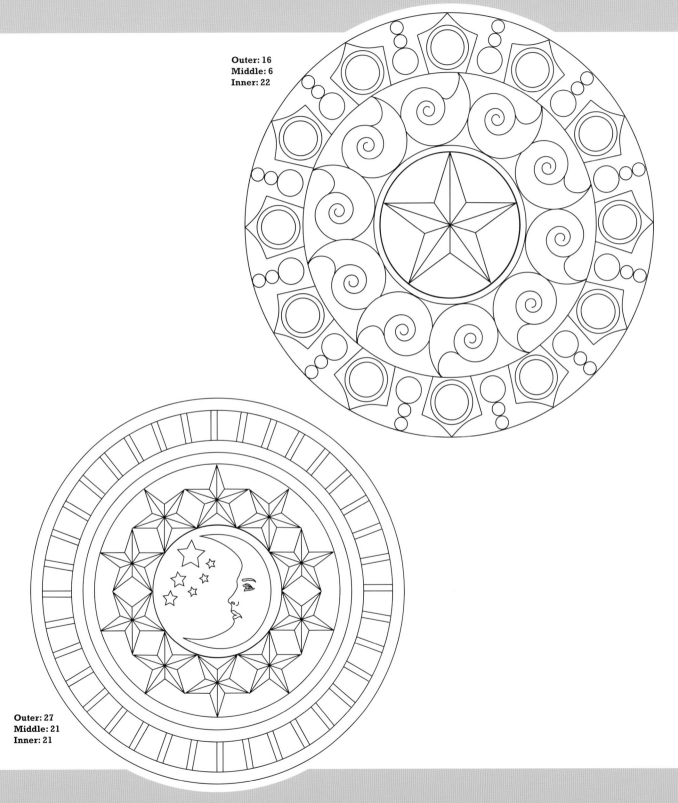

Outer: 16
Middle: 6
Inner: 22

Outer: 27
Middle: 21
Inner: 21

Outer: 47
Middle: 38
Inner: 46

Outer: 66
Middle: 58
Inner: 41

Outer: 45
Middle: 44
Inner: 57

Outer: 70
Middle: 56
Inner: 39

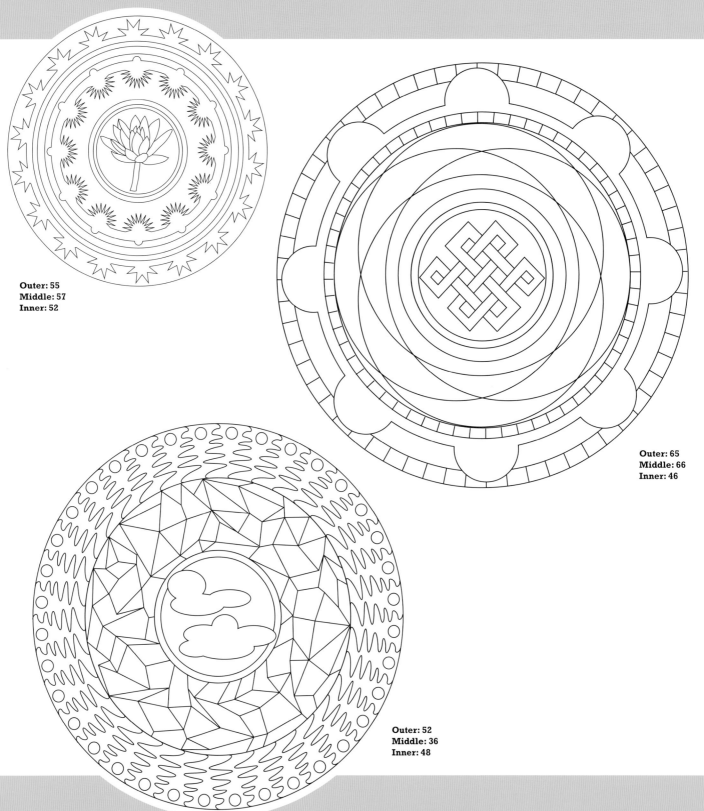

**Outer:** 55
**Middle:** 57
**Inner:** 52

**Outer:** 65
**Middle:** 66
**Inner:** 46

**Outer:** 52
**Middle:** 36
**Inner:** 48

**Outer:** 60
**Middle:** 57
**Inner:** 36

Outer: 50
Middle: 69
Inner: 41

Outer: 39
Middle: 59
Inner: 44

Outer: 53
Middle: 56
Inner: 39

Outer: 56
Middle: 52
Inner: 38

Outer: 86
Middle: 86
Inner: 86

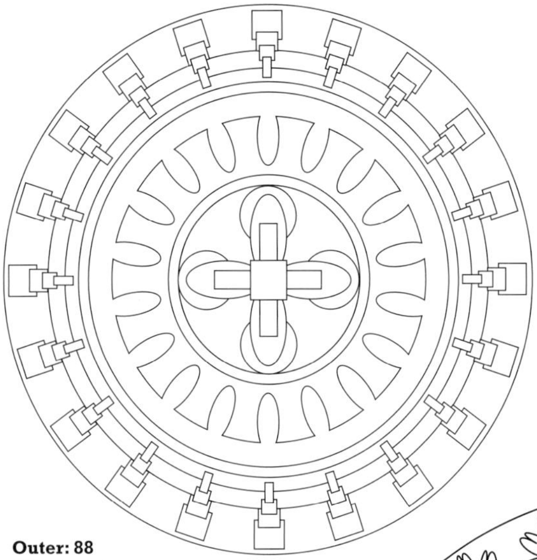

Outer: 88
Middle: 56
Inner: 93

Outer: 90
Middle: 78
Inner: 95

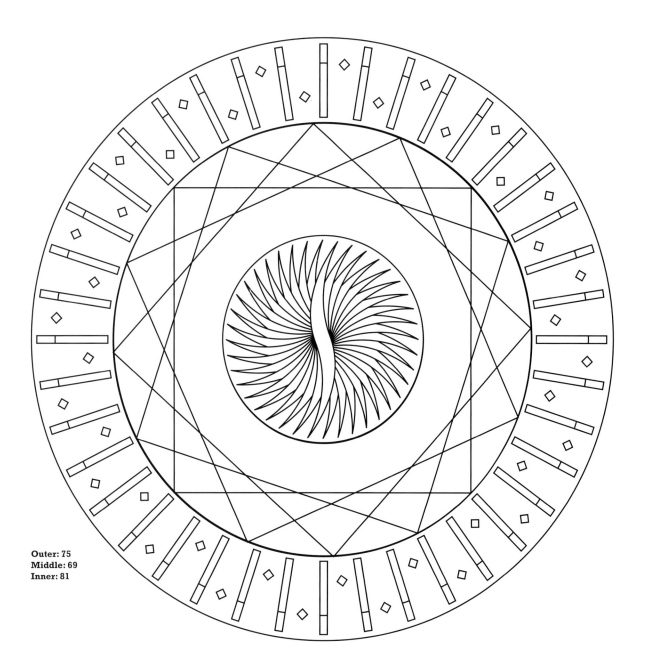

Outer: 75
Middle: 69
Inner: 81

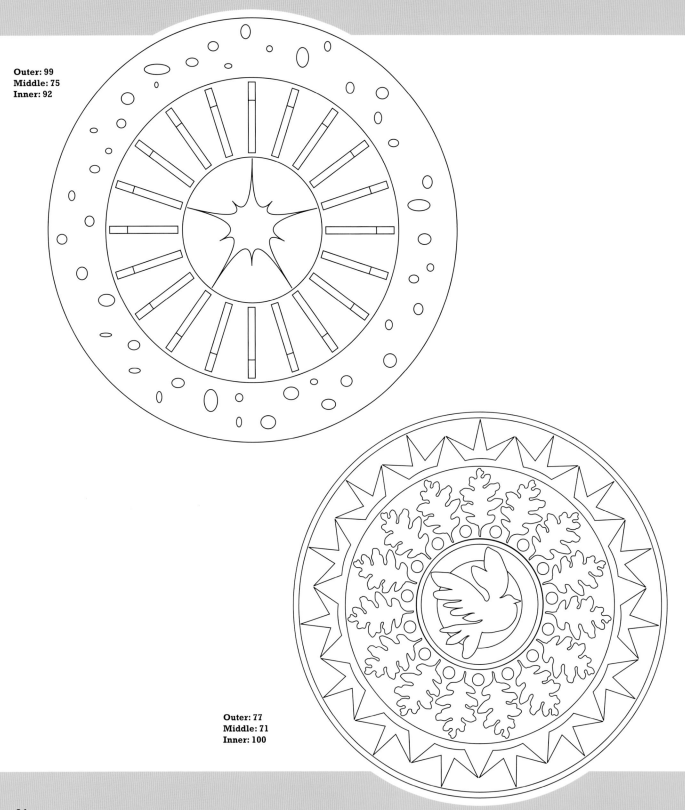

**Outer: 99**
**Middle: 75**
**Inner: 92**

**Outer: 77**
**Middle: 71**
**Inner: 100**

Outer: 83
Middle: 90
Inner: 84

Outer: 98
Middle: 79
Inner: 80

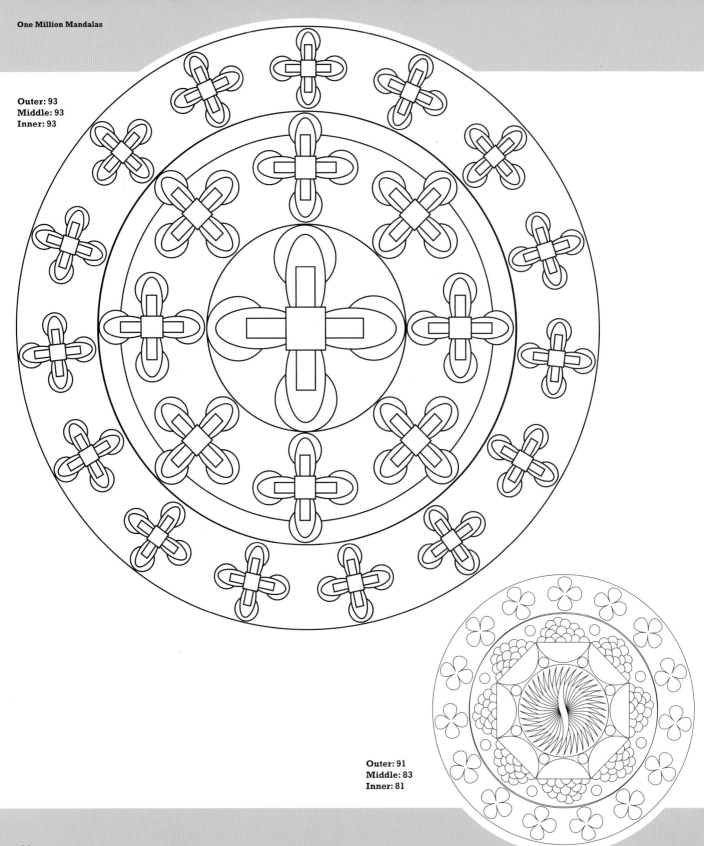

**Outer:** 93
**Middle:** 93
**Inner:** 93

**Outer:** 91
**Middle:** 83
**Inner:** 81

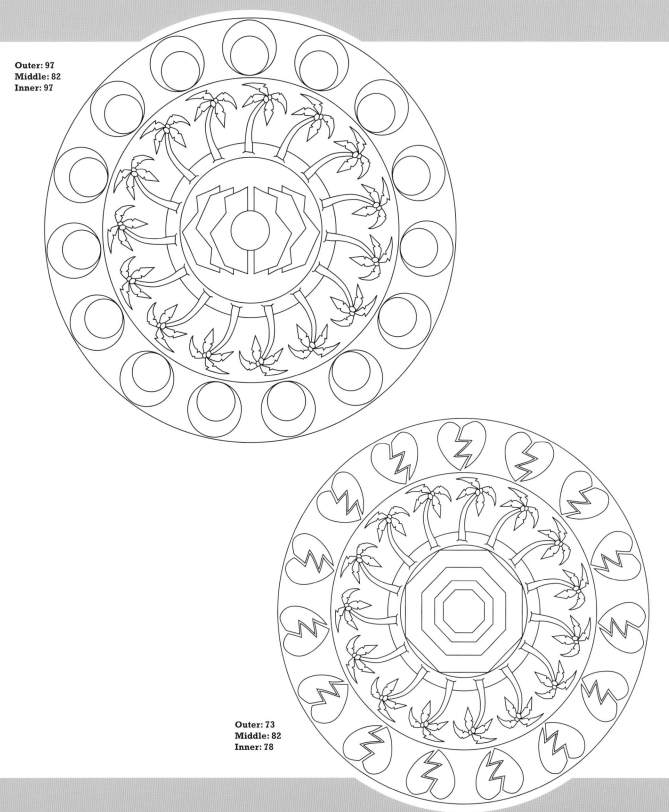

Outer: 97
Middle: 82
Inner: 97

Outer: 73
Middle: 82
Inner: 78

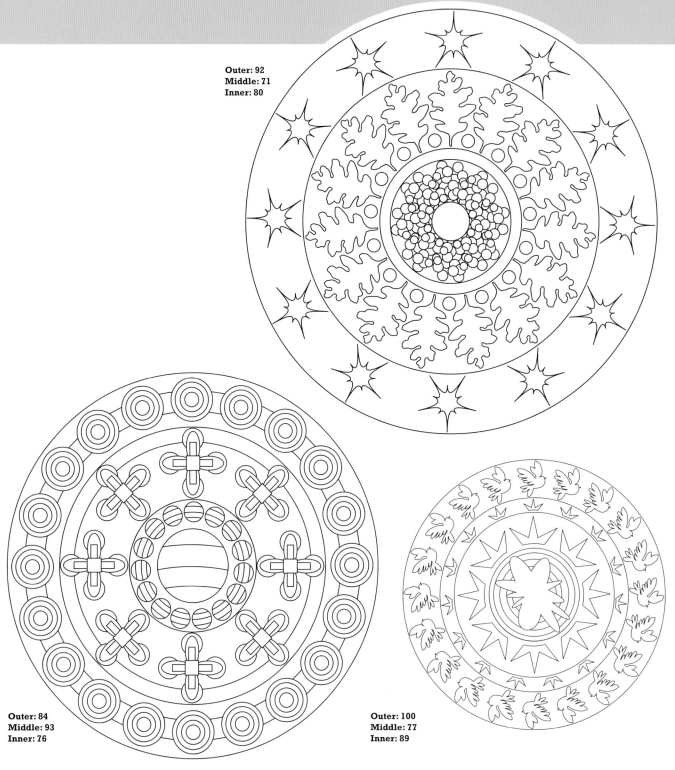

**Outer: 92**
**Middle: 71**
**Inner: 80**

**Outer: 84**
**Middle: 93**
**Inner: 76**

**Outer: 100**
**Middle: 77**
**Inner: 89**

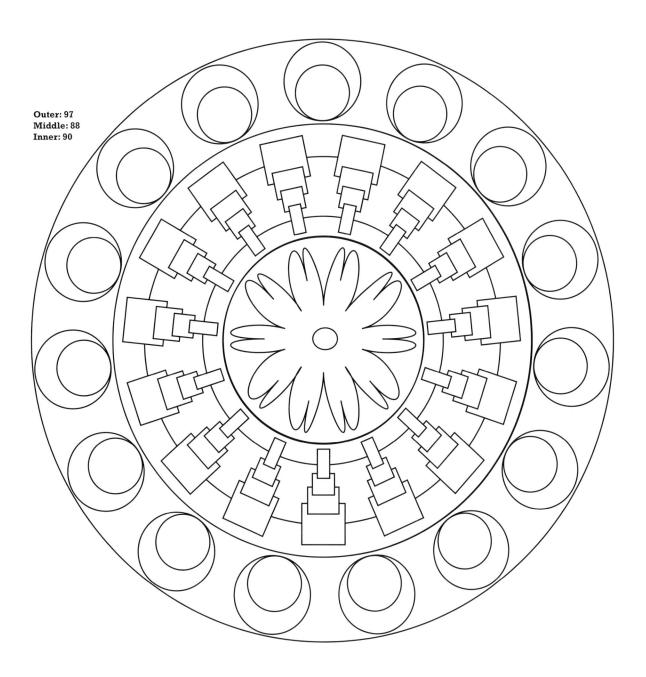

Outer: 97
Middle: 88
Inner: 90

Outer: 96
Middle: 87
Inner: 87

Outer: 87
Middle: 76
Inner: 83

Outer: 96
Middle: 71
Inner: 72

Outer: 100
Middle: 96
Inner: 71

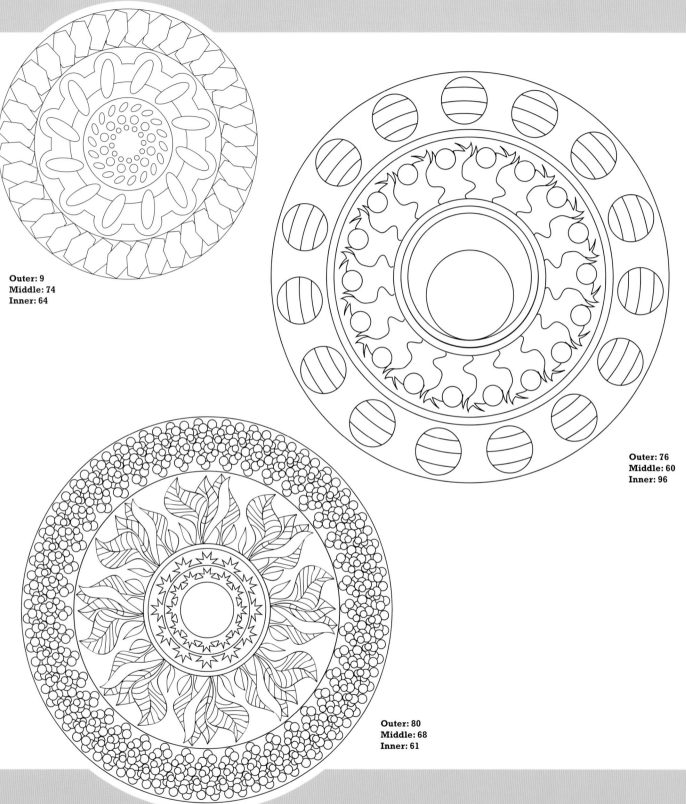

Outer: 9
Middle: 74
Inner: 64

Outer: 76
Middle: 60
Inner: 96

Outer: 80
Middle: 68
Inner: 61

Outer: 57
Middle: 73
Inner: 70

Outer: 44
Middle: 61
Inner: 8

Outer: 94
Middle: 91
Inner: 69

Outer: 100
Middle: 84
Inner: 49

Outer: 78
Middle: 92
Inner: 72

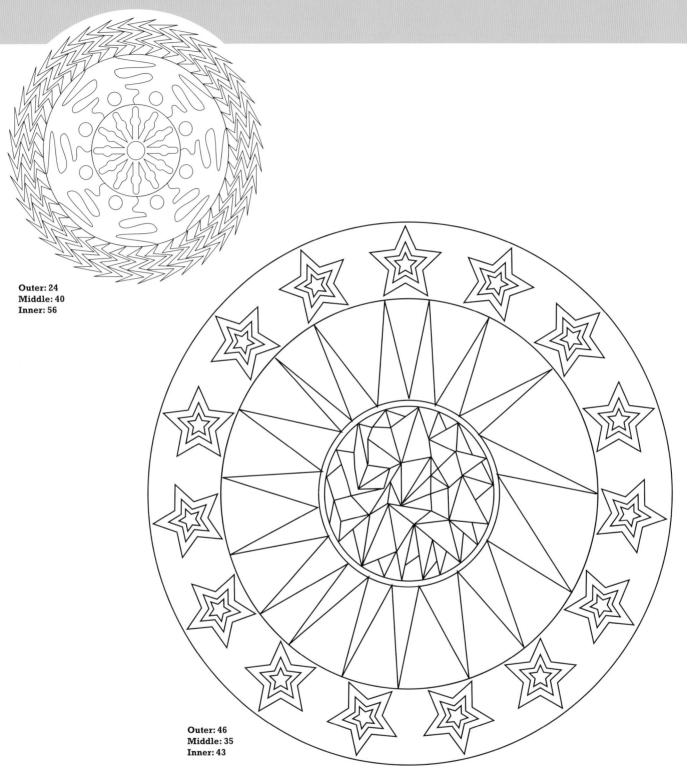

Outer: 24
Middle: 40
Inner: 56

Outer: 46
Middle: 35
Inner: 43

Outer: 45
Middle: 13
Inner: 71

Outer: 69
Middle: 63
Inner: 88

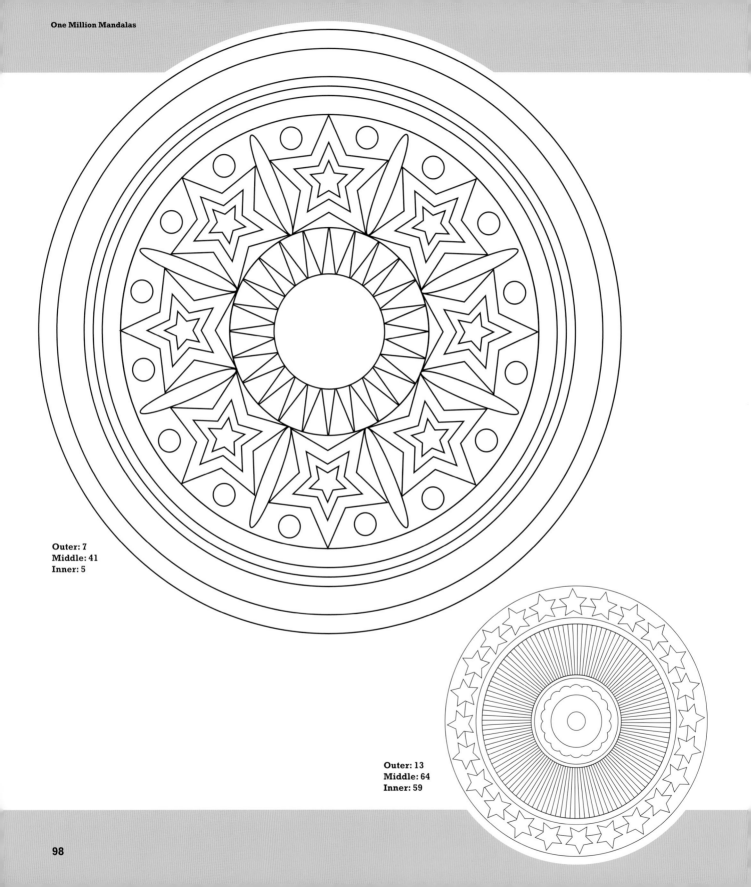

Outer: 7
Middle: 41
Inner: 5

Outer: 13
Middle: 64
Inner: 59

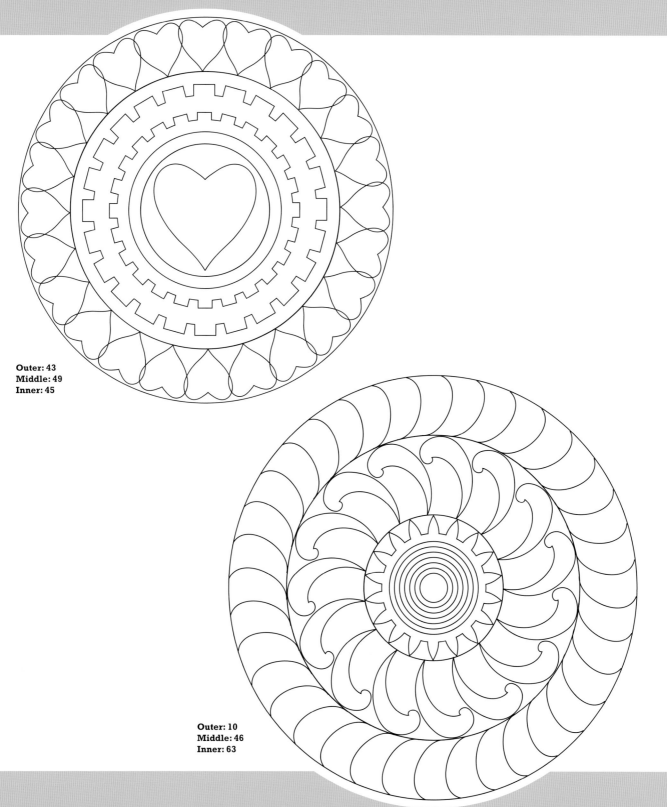

Outer: 43
Middle: 49
Inner: 45

Outer: 10
Middle: 46
Inner: 63

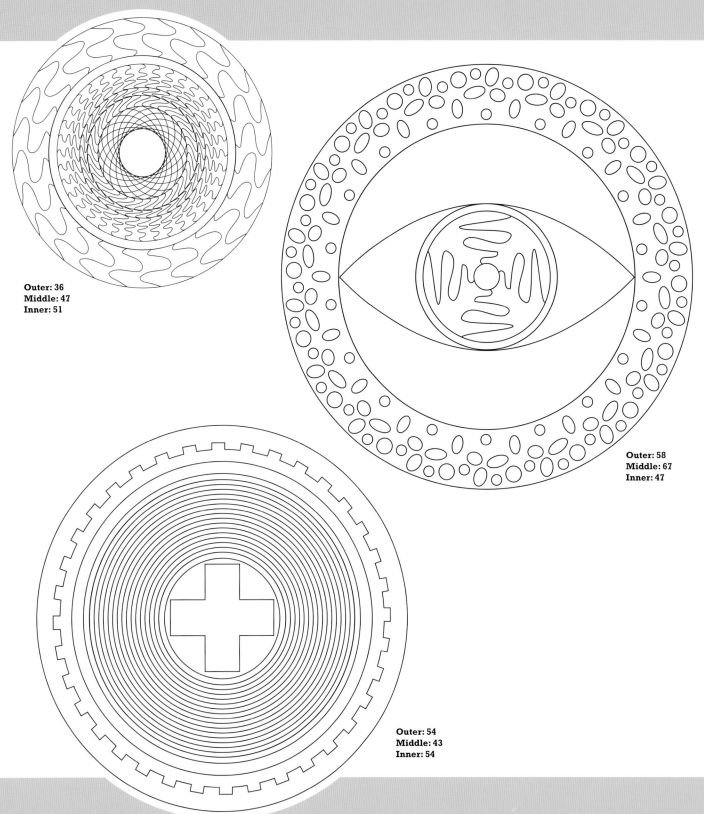

Outer: 36
Middle: 47
Inner: 51

Outer: 58
Middle: 67
Inner: 47

Outer: 54
Middle: 43
Inner: 54

**Outer: 61**
**Middle: 54**
**Inner: 67**

Outer: 6
Middle: 62
Inner: 40

Outer: 38
Middle: 50
Inner: 6

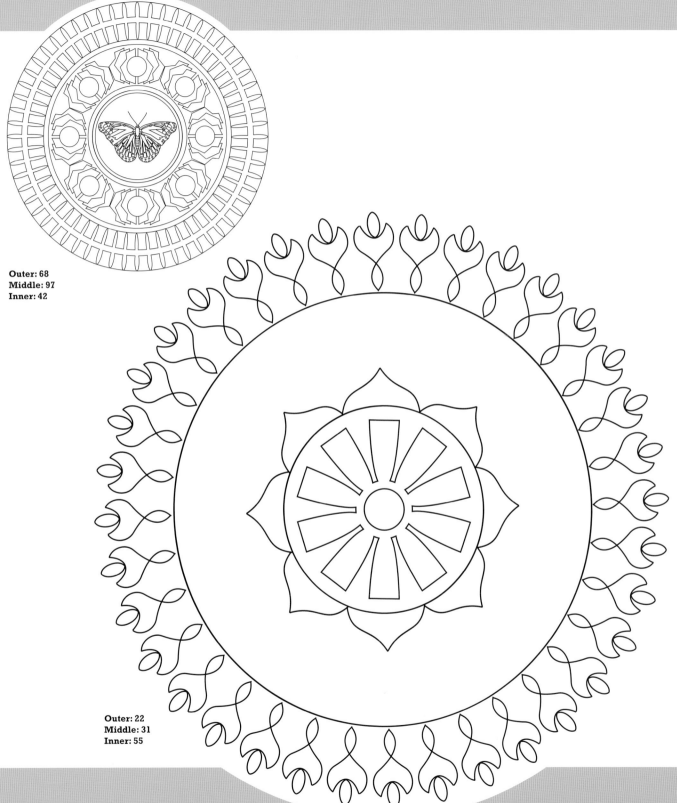

Outer: 68
Middle: 97
Inner: 42

Outer: 22
Middle: 31
Inner: 55

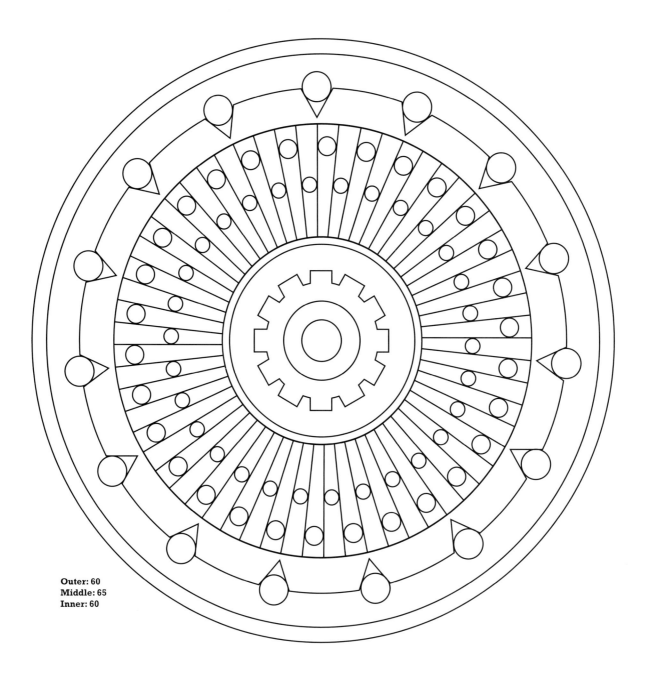

Outer: 60
Middle: 65
Inner: 60

**Outer:** 67
**Middle:** 39
**Inner:** 32

**Outer:** 26
**Middle:** 96
**Inner:** 7

**Outer:** 42
**Middle:** 30
**Inner:** 15

Outer: 41
Middle: 48
Inner: 9

Outer: 91
Middle: 34
Inner: 91

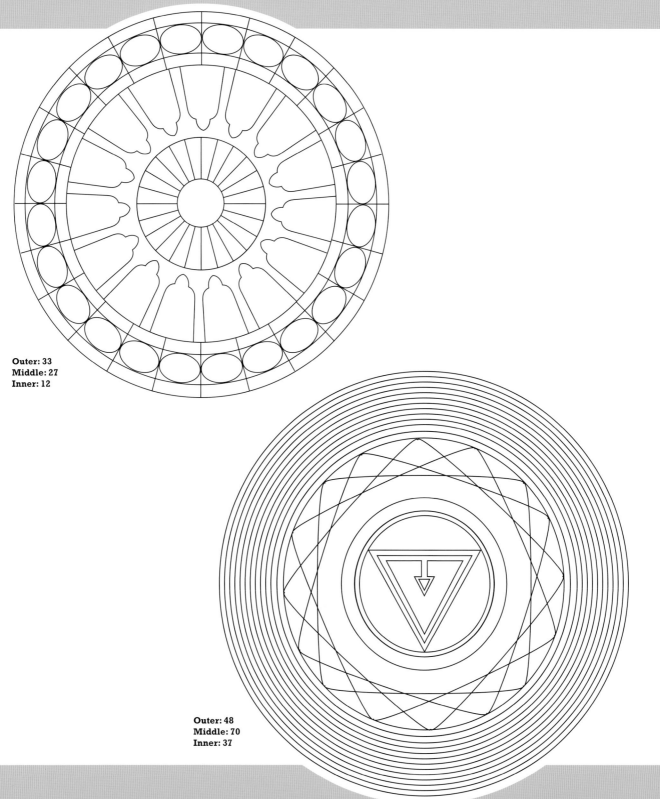

Outer: 33
Middle: 27
Inner: 12

Outer: 48
Middle: 70
Inner: 37

**Outer: 63**
**Middle: 85**
**Inner: 82**

**Outer: 81**
**Middle: 51**
**Inner: 75**

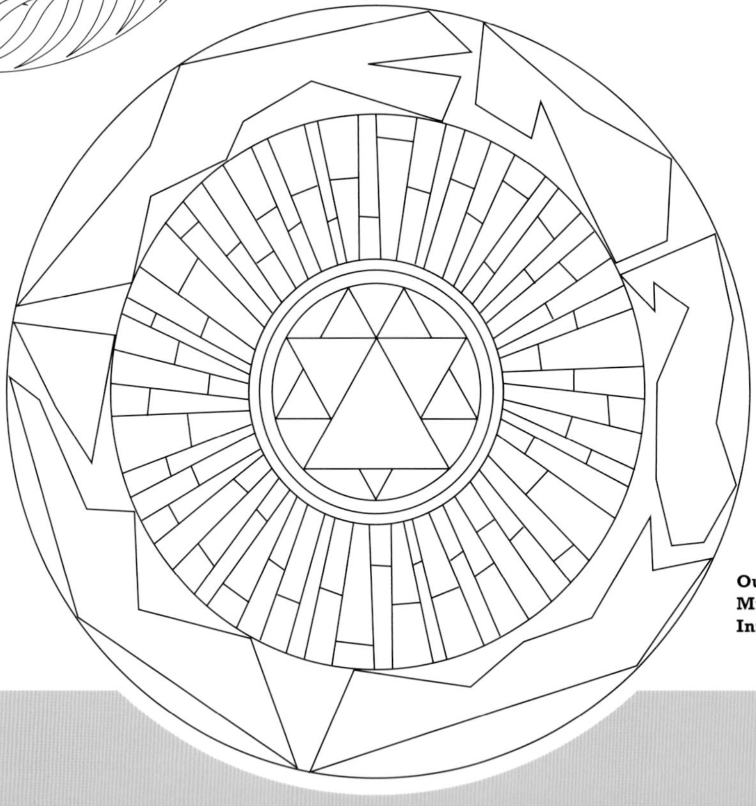

**Outer: 98**
**Middle: 42**
**Inner: 10**

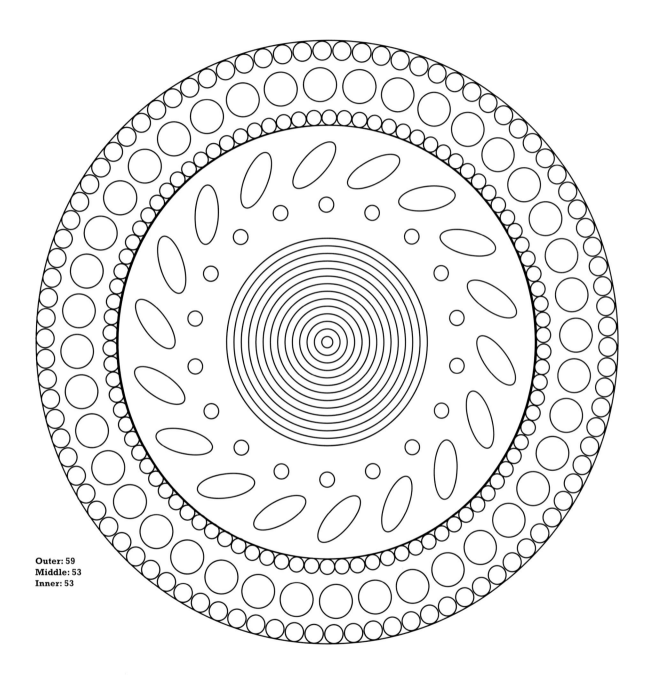

Outer: 59
Middle: 53
Inner: 53

Outer: 82
Middle: 81
Inner: 50

Outer: 74
Middle: 33
Inner: 65

Outer: 50
Middle: 72
Inner: 62

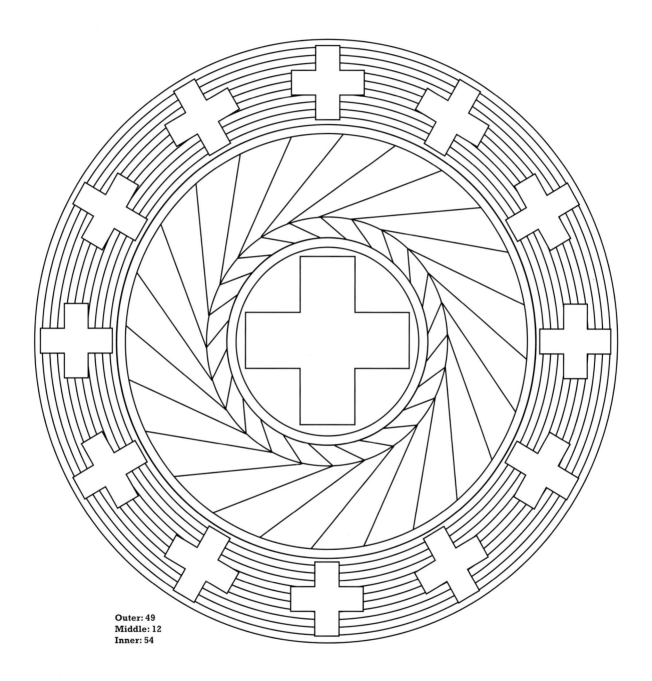

Outer: 49
Middle: 12
Inner: 54

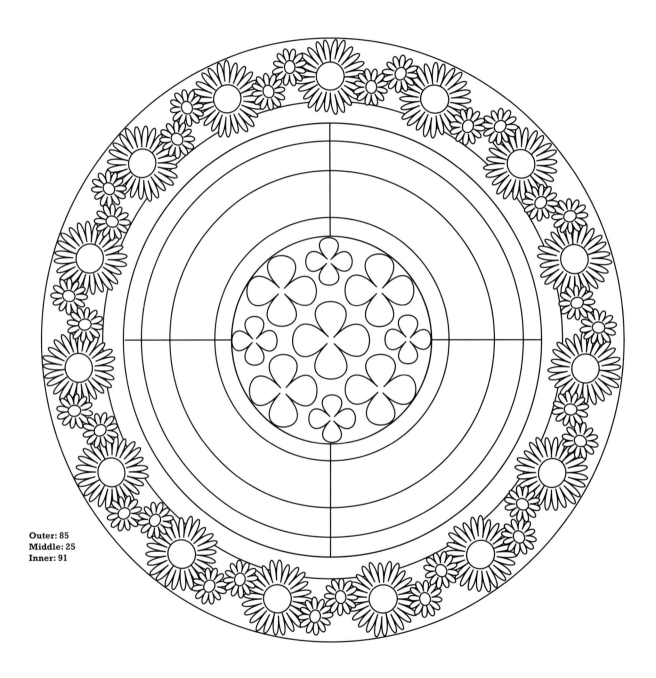

Outer: 85
Middle: 25
Inner: 91

**Outer:** 95
**Middle:** 45
**Inner:** 45

**Outer:** 40
**Middle:** 98
**Inner:** 100

**Outer:** 37
**Middle:** 55
**Inner:** 74

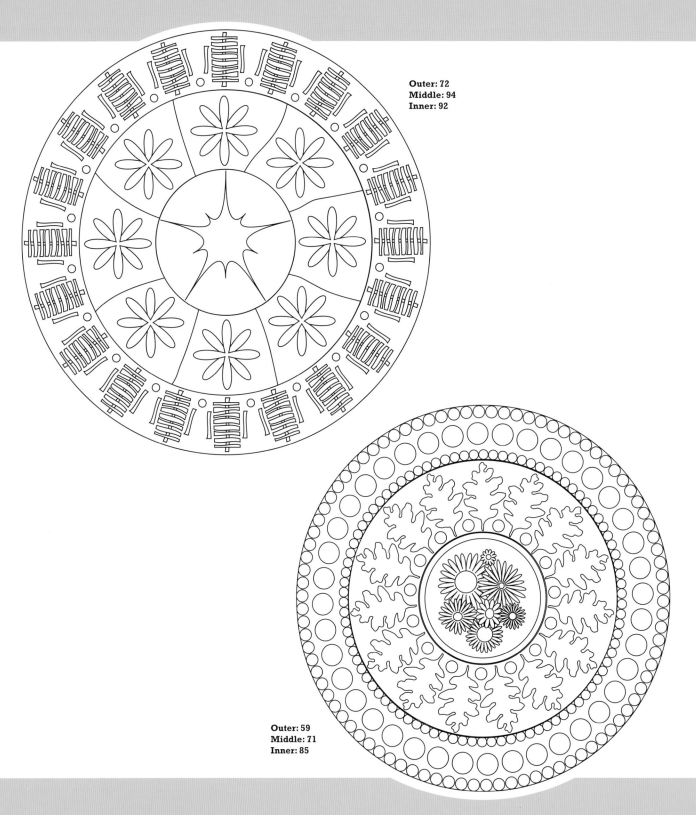

**Outer: 72**
**Middle: 94**
**Inner: 92**

**Outer: 59**
**Middle: 71**
**Inner: 85**

**Outer: 51**
**Middle: 100**
**Inner: 94**

**Outer: 77**
**Middle: 80**
**Inner: 77**

Outer: 70
Middle: 1
Inner: 14

Outer: 6
Middle: 2
Inner: 99

Outer: 84
Middle: 36
Inner: 98

Outer: 42
Middle: 37
Inner: 73

Outer: 89
Middle: 48
Inner: 68

Outer: 36
Middle: 40
Inner: 66

Outer: 22
Middle: 95
Inner: 2

Outer: 62
Middle: 42
Inner: 44

Outer: 79
Middle: 77
Inner: 79

Outer: 81
Middle: 74
Inner: 58

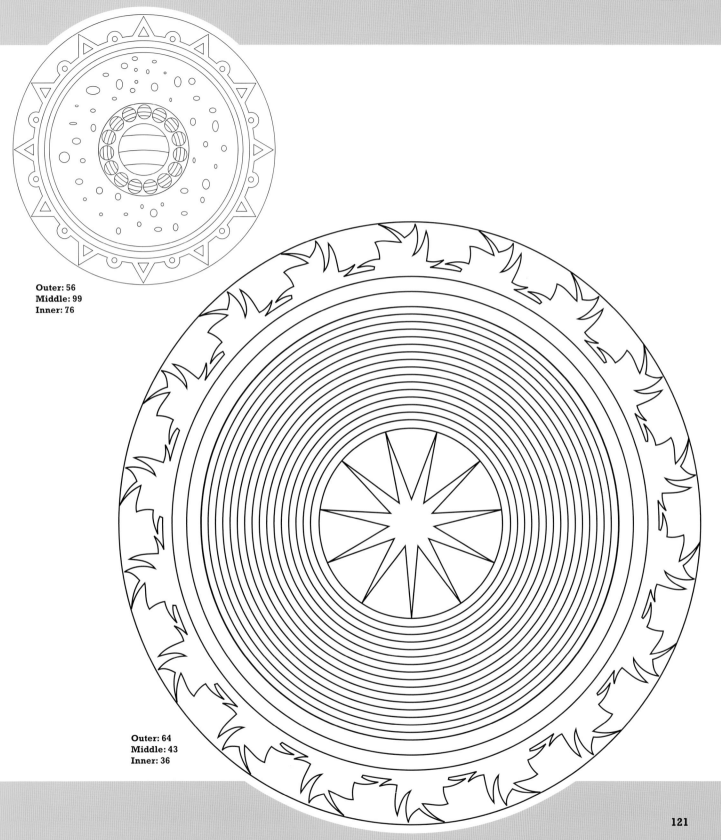

Outer: 56
Middle: 99
Inner: 76

Outer: 64
Middle: 43
Inner: 36

Outer: 81
Middle: 59
Inner: 52

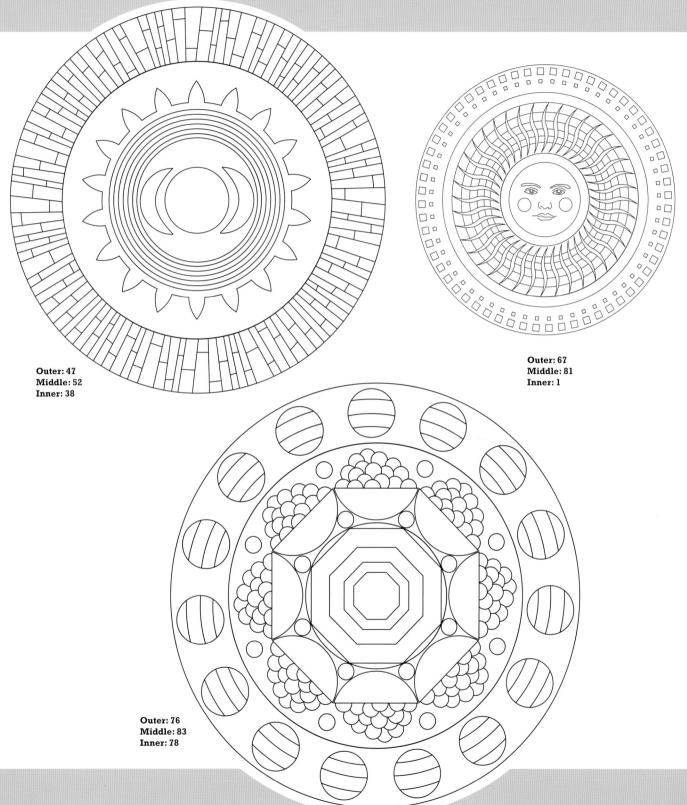

**Outer:** 47
**Middle:** 52
**Inner:** 38

**Outer:** 67
**Middle:** 81
**Inner:** 1

**Outer:** 76
**Middle:** 83
**Inner:** 78

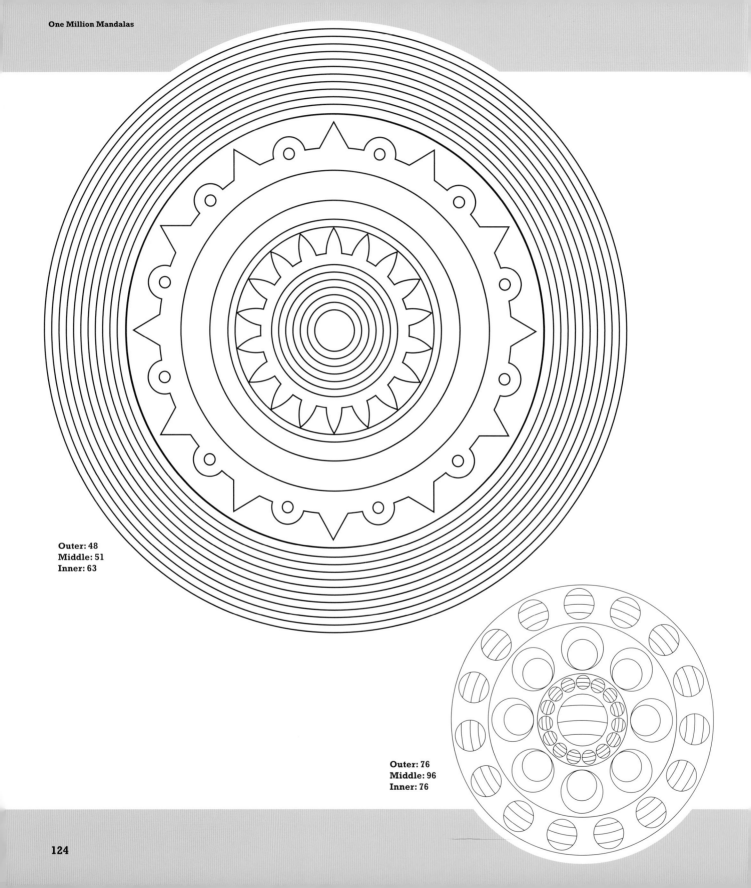

Outer: 48
Middle: 51
Inner: 63

Outer: 76
Middle: 96
Inner: 76

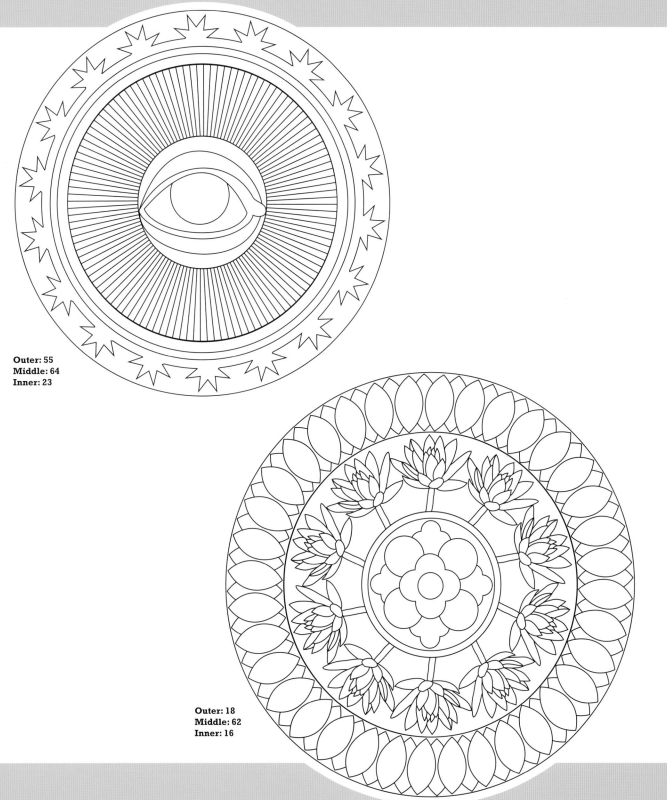

**Outer: 55**
**Middle: 64**
**Inner: 23**

**Outer: 18**
**Middle: 62**
**Inner: 16**

# The Glossary

*Agnus Dei:* A Latin term meaning "Lamb of God" referring to Jesus Christ's sacrifice of his life to atone for the sins of humanity. As a symbol, the Agnus Dei is depicted as a lamb holding a cross, which rests on its shoulder and is held by its right foreleg.

*Alpha and Omega:* The term comes from the phrase "I am the alpha and the omega," an appellation of God in the Book of Revelation, meaning that He is "the first and the last," or "the beginning and the end."

*Buddhism:* Buddhism is a religion based on the teachings of Siddhartha Gautama, commonly known as "The Buddha" who lived in the northeastern part of India and died around 400 BC. The two main forms of Buddhism are Theravada and Mahayana of which the more esoteric form Vajrayana is a part.

*Circle Dance:* The circle dance is probably the oldest known dance formation, and is done without partners to musical accompaniment. Dancing in a circle is an ancient tradition for marking special occasions, strengthening community, and encouraging togetherness. It is found today in many cultures, including Greek, African, Eastern European, Serbian, Irish Celtic, South American, and North American Indian.

*Cosmos:* A cosmos is an orderly or harmonious system and is generally used as a synonym of the word "universe" (see universe).

*Hinduism:* Hinduism is the predominant religion of India, and the third largest religion after Christianity and Islam.

*Hubble Space Telescope:* A space telescope carried into orbit by the Space Shuttle Discovery in April 1990, and named after the American astronomer Edwin Hubble. The Hubble, a collaboration between NASA and the European Space Agency, is positioned outside the Earth's atmosphere allowing it to take extremely sharp images of the universe's most distant objects.

*Jung, Carl:* (1875–1961) a Swiss psychiatrist, and founder of analytical psychology. He promoted understanding the human psyche through the exploration of dreams, symbols, art, mythology, religion, and philosophy.

*Rose Windows:* Large circular stained glass windows divided into segments created with stone mullions and tracery, found in churches with a Gothic architectural style.

*Shiva:* A major Hindu god, and one aspect of Trimurti, a concept in Hinduism in which the cosmic functions of creation, preservation, and destruction are personified by the gods Brahma, the creator; Vishnu, the preserver; and Shiva, the destroyer or transformer. In images, Shiva is often represented as dancing upon Maya, the demon of ignorance in his manifestation of Nataraja, the lord of the dance.

*Spiral Galaxies:* Spiral galaxies consist of a flat, rotating disk of stars, gas, and dust, with a central concentration of stars. They make up approximately 70 percent of galaxies in the local universe.

*Unconscious:* A limited psychological definition of the unconscious is that it is a depository of repressed feelings, such as fear or desires. But the unconscious, or subconscious mind is also the repository of the spiritual and all that is unknown and waiting to be discovered.

*Universe:* Everything that physically exists including all space and time, all forms of matter, energy, and movement, and the physical laws governing them. Some speculate that our universe is just one of many universes that are disconnected from and exist parallel to our own.

*Wooly Mammoth:* The woolly mammoth is an extinct shaggy, elephant-like animal with a trunk and large curving tusks that once populated the Northern areas of Eurasia and America.

## Picture Credits

p 6, Alinta T. Guica & Jupiter Images;
p 7, Jupiter Images;
p 9, NASA;
p 10, Jupiter Images;
p 13, Rafa Irusta.